Building Your own Wealth:
The Ultimate Guide to Achieving Personal finance

Ronald S. Gilbert

THE PURPOSE OF THIS BOOK

'Building Your own Wealth: The Ultimate Guide to Achieving Personal Finance'. This book was written with the aim of helping you achieve financial freedom by providing you with the tools and knowledge you need to take control of your finances.

The book covers a wide range of topics, including budgeting, saving, investing, and building wealth over the long term. It is designed to be a comprehensive guide that will take you through the basics of personal finance and give you the confidence and skills you need to make informed financial decisions.

Whether you are just starting out on your financial journey or looking to take your finances to the next level, this book is here to help you. With practical tips and expert advice, you'll learn how to build wealth, manage your money, and achieve your financial goals.

I hope this book will be a valuable resource for you and help you to achieve financial independence. Thank you for choosing to read 'Building Your own Wealth: The Ultimate Guide to Achieving Personal Finance'.

TABLE OF CONTENT

Creating a strong brand
Marketing strategies for growing your business

Understanding expansion strategies
Franchising and other expansion models

Building and managing your investment portfolio
Tax planning strategies
Asset protection strategies

THE IMPORTANCE OF BUILDING WEALTH

Achieving financial security and independence requires building wealth. It entails developing a stable financial future for your family, your community, and yourself. It is impossible to exaggerate the value of accumulating money since it creates a solid base for long-term success and financial security.

The ability to protect oneself from unanticipated events like medical problems, job loss, or economic downturns is one of the main benefits of generating wealth. Building money allows you to accumulate a cash reserve that you may use when necessary, easing financial pressure and giving you peace of mind. Since you may rely on your own resources rather than being compelled to rely on government assistance or other types of aid, this safety net also helps you weather economic storms.

Financial freedom that comes from building money enables you to follow your hobbies and interests without worrying about your financial situation. Having the money to do so may make a huge impact whether you want to start a business, explore the world, or seek further education. Moreover, this flexibility gives you the chance to support important organizations and give back to your community.

Wealth creation also leaves a legacy for future generations. You may leave your money and expertise to your children and grandkids by laying a solid financial foundation. As a result, people may go on their individual financial paths with the information and tools necessary to attain financial stability and success.

There are several methods and approaches for accumulating riches, and each person must choose the one that suits them the most. Making a budget, cutting costs, investing in stocks or real estate, and beginning a business are a few typical ways. Regardless of the strategy, accumulating money necessitates self-control, concentration, and a readiness to accept short-term sacrifices in exchange for long-term benefit.

The development of several revenue sources is a crucial component of wealth accumulation. By varying the sources of your income, you may lower your risk and boost your chances of long-term development. This might entail buying stocks or real estate, beginning a side company, or looking at passive income options like leasing out real estate or buying a business.

Having an abundance-focused attitude as opposed to a scarcity-focused one is another crucial component in building wealth. This entails putting opportunities first rather than constraints and looking for methods to add value and make money. It also entails being prepared to weigh the risks and admit failing.

In conclusion, accumulating wealth is a necessary step toward obtaining financial stability and independence. It gives you the financial flexibility to follow your passions, a safety net in times of need, and chances to give back to your community. Everyone can start creating wealth now and ensure a better financial future for themselves and their loved ones by adopting an abundant mentality, diversifying their sources of income, and making wise financial decisions.

CHAPTER 1:

UNDERSTANDING PERSONAL FINANCE

The basics of personal finance:

Personal finance might appear quite frightening since it encompasses all of the financial decisions you make during your life. But rest assured—it doesn't have to be difficult!

The fundamentals of personal finance are extremely doable tasks that you can and will master when you break them down. So let's get going.

You must first establish a budget. Why? Your ability to stick to a budget will serve as the base for all other personal financial practices. That's because creating a budget simply entails setting a plan for your money, including every dollar that comes in and every dollar that leaves your account. Here is how to go about it.

List your income first. Any money you expect to earn that month is your income. It covers take-home wages as well as any earnings from side jobs.

After that, take away all of your costs. Plan for your Four Walls: food, utilities, housing, and transportation once you've given and saved. Include your regular monthly costs next, such as insurance and child care. Include extras like dining out and entertainment if there is any money left.

Give yourself a high five if, after deducting all of your costs, you still have money left over. Don't, however, treat that cash as "extra." Use it to further your present financial objectives, such as debt repayment or saving.

Create a budget right away using EveryDollar!
If the result is negative, you must reduce spending until your income less your costs equal zero.

The following is the next phase in budgeting: Monitor your spending (which, by the way, is one of our top personal finance tips, period). Do it for the whole month. This implies that every dollar that enters or exits your bank account needs to be recorded in your budget and allocated to the appropriate budget line.

This is how you keep track of your expenditures, prevent overspending, and develop sound financial practices. Because monitoring is the accountability and your budget is the strategy.

Lastly, make a fresh budget each month (before the month begins). To be prepared for what's ahead, don't forget to include any costs that are unique to a given month.
Saving for significant purchases or twice-yearly expenses.
Not all of your expenses take place on a consistent, monthly schedule. You should gradually accumulate money for these via a sinking fund, like in the case of.

Tires on your automobile are deteriorating; start saving for replacements.
Divide the amount of your twice-yearly insurance payment and set aside a portion of it each month.
You pay an annual fee for something; again, split the fee into equal monthly payments.
Save money until you can make the complete payment if you want to work on house repairs or get new furnishings.
You may budget for significant and semiannual costs over time to spread out the cost by setting aside money in a sinking fund. This will prevent an unexpected expense from blowing your budget.

Create a fund for emergencies.

Your grandma advised you to put money aside for a rainy day. Why? Because. It. Pours. We refer to it as an emergency fund, but she dubbed it a rainy-day fund.

Start with a $1,000 startup budget. Use the additional money you were spending on debt payments to start your fully funded emergency fund when you have paid off all of your debt (more on that later). How? Read on.

Consider your budget first. How much does it cost to run your home every month? What necessary expenses and commitments would you still have to fulfill if your income disappeared?

In case of an emergency, you should have enough money saved to pay for those costs for three to six months. It translates to three months for those with two incomes and six months for those with just one.

Keep this money accessible, or keep it liquid. Your emergency fund is insurance, not a long-term investment. And it must be available when you need it. It does not, however, follow that you should wedge it between your mattress and box spring. (It seems a little too open.)

Put the money in a straightforward money market account so you may access it by writing a cheque or visiting an ATM. In this manner, it won't be a temptation when summer vacation time rolls around if it's not there with your usual money. No matter how much you want for salt air, it is not an emergency.

You will be prepared for anything that comes your way since you have an emergency fund that is filled. You'll be able to sleep better with that level of financial stability than you can during any seashore snooze.

Save money for retirement
The process of saving for retirement is simpler than you would imagine. Let's start by discussing how much money to put in. Once you have paid off all of your debt and built up the fully loaded emergency fund we just discussed, you can start saving 15% of your salary for retirement when you follow the Baby Steps.

Here's how to join in when you get to that point: Check to see whether your workplace offers a matching 401(k) or 403(b). If they do, use that free money by contributing to your 401(k) up to the company match!

The second step is to form a Roth IRA if you already have a standard 401(k) via your employer (which is funded with pretax funds); this way, your future growth, and withdrawals will be tax-free!

Nevertheless, because the Roth offers such a significant tax benefit, Uncle Sam caps it at $6,500 in 2023 (or $7,500 if you're 50 or older).

To return to your 401(k) and continue making investments there if you reach the maximum of that and still haven't reached 15%.

You should distribute your contributions across the four categories of mutual funds in both the 401(k) and Roth IRA: growth, growth and income, aggressive growth, and international.

In this manner, you avoid putting all of your eggs in one basket. Diversification in the context of investment refers to this and is both prudent and less hazardous.

Check out our R: IQ retirement assessment if you're attempting to determine how much money you need to save to retire on your terms. Based on your age, salary, and desired retirement lifestyle, it does the arithmetic for you and displays the precise monthly investment amount.

Acquire the Best Insurance

Indeed, insurance is a lot of fun. Right? I guess not for the majority of us. But that doesn't lessen how important it is. Also, you can be aware that you need insurance but be unsure of the type, cost, or provider.

Don't be concerned. The eight forms of insurance you require are summarized in the following manner:

Term life insurance: Life insurance is all about securing your family's safety and protection. A 15- or 20-year term life insurance coverage is required. Average term life insurance premiums are frequently less expensive than average whole life insurance premiums. Furthermore, unlike whole life, which poses as investment insurance but offers a poor rate of return, term life isn't a complete rip-off. (Thanks, but no.)

Car Insurance: In general, you need full coverage, which covers liability, collision, and comprehensive, for the most beneficial auto insurance. Consider eliminating collision if your car is older and paid for. There are a few other optional varieties and add-ons that your state could mandate you get. To discuss your alternatives and obtain the best prices, it is a good idea to speak with an independent insurance agent.

Homeowners or renters insurance: If you own a house, be sure to obtain extended dwelling coverage and inquire about flood and earthquake insurance with your insurance agent. Tenants, if your belongings are lost in a fire, a burglary, or another tragedy, your landlord is not obligated to replace them. To pay for the expense of replacing your belongings, you need renters insurance.

Medical Insurance If you don't have health insurance, one serious medical emergency might practically put you out of business. But if you're concerned about the expense, think about getting health insurance with a large deductible and a Health Savings Account (HSA). This is a fantastic method to be protected in an emergency without having to pay a very high monthly premium.

Long-Term Disability Insurance: Invest in long-term disability insurance to help replace your income if an illness or accident prevents you from working any longer. As much insurance as you can acquire, around 60–70% of your salary, is what we advise. You do not need temporary disability. (You'll be covered there by your fully funded emergency fund.)

Long-Term Care Insurance: Don't count on Medicare to cover your expenses if you wind up requiring long-term care in your elder years. Plan to purchase long-term care insurance that includes in-home care when you turn 60. (not just nursing homes).

Identity theft protection: Pay attention: Anybody may become a victim of identity theft, and it might take years to fully recover on your own. You must safeguard against identity theft! Be sure the plan you choose provides services for both protection and recuperation. You require Social Security number tracking, change of address tracking, compensation, and recovery services. It implies that when you need help, someone else will put in all those hours to bring your life back in order.

Umbrella Insurance: If your net worth exceeds $500,000, you need umbrella insurance to safeguard your residence and savings from liability claims that go over and beyond the limits of your house and car insurance policies. Not enjoyable to consider, but essential!

That's a lot; oh my. So don't worry—having enough insurance doesn't need you to be an expert in the field. (Goodness, please!)

But, you must take the initiative.

Fundamentals of Personal Finance

Make a Will

You must have a will, we'll simply say it right now. It's not an enjoyable aspect, but it's a vital element of putting your finances in order and being a responsible adult.

If you don't take control of this situation, the government will decide what happens to your possessions, your money, and your family.

Making important judgments on something you initially don't want to think about is indeed a lot to cope with. Yet, you need a strong will.

Choose a trustworthy, reasonably priced internet supplier who streamlines the procedure and eliminates legalese. (By simple, we mean work on the paperwork while still in your jammies.) Don't put it off, then. Get a will right away.

Clear Your Debt

Some people believe that taking on debt helps them establish credit or earn expensive flyer miles. In actuality, debt is a burden that drags you down and prevents you from moving forward. Just 24% of Americans reported reducing their debt as of June 2022, according to our study, and one in five had increased their debt since that month.

And regrettably, stress and debt go hand in hand. It can be the case since debt prevents you from ever moving up. With payments for something you purchased months or even years ago, it keeps a portion of your money captive each month. That type of tension is not necessary for you.

Here's some crucial personal financial advice: Your biggest asset for accumulating money is your income. You reclaim your paycheck once you have paid off your debt. You receive a refund for the additional payments you made on your loan.

What might you buy with that more cash? Use it to create budget space. Utilize it to further your financial objectives, such as retirement and savings! Utilize it for yourself.

"A tool is not debt. Your salary is. Bring it back."

Make informed housing choices
We could complicate this one. But we don't do that. Making personal finance understandable and straightforward is our forte.

Therefore, these are the three key things to keep in mind when you're considering purchasing a home.

Limit the amount of your monthly take-home income that you spend on housing to 25%. If you obtain a mortgage, your total monthly payment, PMI, real estate taxes, insurance, and any HOA dues shouldn't exceed 25%. (Renters are subject to the same restriction—their rent and any related costs shouldn't total more than 25%.)
If you're going to acquire a mortgage, get a conventional loan with a 15-year fixed rate. (In comparison to pricey FHA, VA, and 30-year loans, you'll save thousands.)
Before you purchase a property, save aside at least 20% of the purchase price as a down payment to avoid PMI costs.
(First-time buyers can save for a lesser down payment, such as 5–10%, but you'll still have to pay PMI.)
If you don't adhere to those three rules, you risk becoming "house poor," which means that even

while your home may be fantastic, it consumes so much of your income that you struggle with money in other areas.

Obtain a Financial Game Plan.
Personal finance is therefore somewhat complex. Yet both major and minor financial decisions may be improved. All you need is the appropriate strategy.

You can discover all you need to know about sound money management later on in this book. This course will guide you through all the fundamentals of personal finance, from setting up a budget and eliminating debt to setting aside money for unplanned expenses and investing for the future.

CREATING A BUDGET
How to create a budget:

  Make a spreadsheet for it or Use an app for budgeting.
Compute your whole income (net).
Calculate your spending and enter your daily costs.
Plan ahead
Change your spending habits to keep them under your budget.

Establish attainable objectives that you can monitor.

Make a spreadsheet for it or Use an app for budgeting:
Well, this is a simple step to do. Without really constructing "the area" where you'll describe your income and spending, it is impossible to make a budget. Choose a tool that is simple to use and readily available. Some individuals dislike spreadsheets at all costs, yet a tool with rows and columns for organizing data works just fine. I'll suggest that you avoid using a pen and paper for this because you'll have to start over the day it goes missing.

When you first start, I'll suggest that you only make a budget for one month; anything longer can become overwhelming. Create a weekly or monthly budget to start.

Compute your whole income (net):
Your wage is one source of money to eliminate if you work a 9 to 5 job. Don't stop there, though. Name EVERYTHING you've earned money from over the previous few months, including side hustles, parental vex money (if you're a trust fund

kid), etc. On the other hand, if your wage is the only source of income, just say such.

Calculate your spending and enter your daily costs: Include Anything you can think of that you typically spend money on in your budget. Nothing should be left out, not even the $5 you spent (if there is such a thing in this x3 economy).
Provide an estimate of the amount you believe you will spend on each item after creating the list. For each expense, the average monthly cost will be calculated.

Do the math to determine the difference between your income and expenses.
Calculating the gap between your income and expenses is an important step in developing a budget. After you're finished, if your costs are significantly less than your income, you've reached a decent point. My expected spending was greater than my estimated income when I made my first budget, so I realized I had to make adjustments.

Make set and discretionary categories for your spending.
Transportation, debt, food, rent, light bills, and other items fall under the category of fixed expenditures. These are necessary items. Things

that are significant to you but not as significant as your fixed spending will fall under the category of discretionary expenses. This may include regular movie times, travel schedules, etc., and they might be postponed. Delaying your rent, light bill, or loan payments (if any) will lead to tears, though.

Enter your daily expenses here.
The preceding point, where you estimated how much you used to spend on an item, is distinct from this. Here, you must enter every dollar spent each day in your budget.

Expense	Amount ($)
Transportation to and from work.	2500
Food	1800
Data subscription	5,000
Sent money to younger bro	2000
Total	11,300

I've discovered that filling this in daily, or at the very least early the next day, works best. This is because the brain can only take so much. Documenting this daily will ensure that you don't forget anything, giving you accurate numbers at the end of the week or month - depending on the timeframe you want to follow. To improve accuracy, divide these expenses into cash and bank debits.

Plan Ahead:

This is the point at which everything comes together: what you spend versus what you want to spend. Use the variable and fixed expenses you accumulated to estimate how much you'll spend in the coming months. After that, compare it to your net income and priorities. Consider establishing specific (and reasonable) spending limits for each category of expenses.

You may want to further divide your expenses into things you must have and things you want to have. For example, if you drive to work every day, gasoline is considered a necessity. A monthly music subscription, on the other hand, may be considered a want. This distinction is significant when you're looking for ways to redirect money toward your financial goals.

Change your spending habits to keep them under your budget.

You can make any necessary adjustments now that you've documented your income and spending so that you don't overspend and have money to put toward your goals. Cuts should be made initially in the area of your "wants." Can you forego movie night in favor of seeing a movie at home? If you've already reduced your spending on desires, examine your expenditure on monthly payments. Scrutiny reveals that a "need" may just be "hard to part with."

If the figures still don't add up, consider altering your fixed expenses. Might you, for example, save more money by comparing vehicle and homeowners insurance rates? Such selections include significant trade-offs, so carefully consider your options.

Remember that even tiny saves may build up to a significant amount of money. You might be shocked at how much money you can save by making little changes one at a time.

And Regularly review your budget. After you've established your budget, it's critical to check it and your expenditures regularly to ensure you're on track. A few aspects of your budget are fixed: you may get a raise, your costs might alter, or you might attain a goal and wish to set a new one. Whatever the cause, get into the practice of checking in with your budget regularly by following the steps outlined above.

Establish attainable objectives that you can monitor:
Now that you've assessed your spending patterns and determined if you're Excellent, Good, Average, or Bad... You must then pick what to double down on and what to abandon. Establish explicit targets and track their progress.

Make a list of your short- and long-term financial goals before you begin combing through the data you've collected. Short-term goals should be completed within one to three years and may include things like putting up an emergency fund or paying off credit card debt. Long-term objectives, like saving for retirement or your child's education, might take decades to achieve. Note that your objectives do not have to be etched in stone, but knowing what they are will help drive you to stay within your budget. For example, if you know you're saving for a trip, it may be simpler to cut back on spending.

WHAT IS THE 50/30/20 RULE?

In her book, All Your Worth: The Ultimate Lifetime Money Plan, U.S. Senator Elizabeth Warren popularized the 50/20/30 budget rule. The rule is to divide your after-tax income into three categories of spending: needs, wants, and savings.

This simple rule can assist you in creating a reasonable budget that you can stick to over time to meet your financial objectives.

According to the rule, you should spend up to 50% of your after-tax income on necessities and obligations that you must have or fulfill.
The remaining half should be divided as follows: 20% for savings and debt repayment, and 30% for anything else you desire.
The rule is a template designed to assist individuals in managing their money and saving for emergencies and retirement.
Americans have a massive amount of debt, totaling $14.9 trillion as of the third quarter of 2020.

50%: NEEDS
Needs are bills that must be paid and items that are required for survival. Rent or mortgage payments, car payments, groceries, insurance, health care,

minimum debt payments, and utilities are examples. These are your "must-have" items. Extras such as HBO, Netflix, Starbucks, and dining out are not included in the "needs" category.

Half of your after-tax income should be sufficient to meet your needs and obligations. If you spend more than that on needs, you will have to either cut back on wants or downsize your lifestyle, perhaps to a smaller home or a less expensive car. Perhaps carpooling or taking public transportation to work is an option, as is cooking at home more frequently.

30%: WANTS
Wants are all the things you buy that aren't necessary. This includes outings to the movies and dinner, a new handbag, sporting event tickets, vacations, the latest electronic gadget, and ultra-high-speed Internet. When it comes down to it, anything in the "wants" bucket is optional. You can exercise at home instead of going to the gym, cook instead of eating out, or watch sports on TV instead of purchasing game tickets.

This category also includes upgrade decisions such as choosing a more expensive steak over a cheaper hamburger, purchasing a Mercedes over a more economical Honda, or deciding between watching television for free via an antenna or paying for cable TV. Wants are all the little extras you buy to make your life more enjoyable and entertaining.

SAVINGS: 20%
Finally, try to set aside 20% of your net earnings for savings and investments. This includes putting money into an emergency fund in a bank savings account, contributing to a mutual fund account through an IRA, and investing in the stock market. You should have at least three months' worth of emergency savings on hand in case you lose your job or something unexpected happens. After that, concentrate on retirement and other long-term financial goals.

If you ever need to use your emergency funds, the first thing you should do with any extra money is replenish the emergency fund account.
Debt repayment can also be included in savings. While minimum payments are considered "needs," any additional payments reduce the principal and future interest owed, making the savings.

THE VALUE OF SAVINGS
Americans are famously lousy at saving, yet the country is deeply in debt. Americans have $14.9

trillion in overall debt as of the third quarter of 2020, including $756 billion in credit card debt.

In January 2022, the personal savings rate was 6.4%.

The 50-20-30 rule is meant to assist individuals in managing their after-tax income, particularly to keep cash on hand for emergencies and retirement savings. Every household should prioritize the establishment of an emergency fund in the event of job loss, unexpected medical bills, or any other unforeseen financial obligation. If an emergency fund is exhausted, a family should prioritize replacing it.

Investing in retirement is particularly important since people live longer lives. Determining your retirement needs and working toward that objective from a young age can assure a pleasant retirement.

In conclusion

Saving money is difficult, and life frequently throws unexpected bills our way. Those that adhere to the 50-20-30 rule have a strategy for managing their after-tax income. If they discover that their spending on wants exceeds 30%, they can identify strategies to cut those expenses, allowing monies to be directed to more critical areas such as emergency reserves and retirement.

Life should be enjoyed, and living like a Spartan is not encouraged, but having a plan and following it will help you to cover your bills, save for retirement, and do the things that make you happy.

EMERGENCY AND RETIREMENT SAVINGS

When it comes to personal money, many conflicting goals might make deciding where to spend your efforts challenging. One of the most difficult decisions many individuals have is deciding between accumulating emergency funds and working toward their retirement objectives. So, which should you prioritize first?

To answer this question, it's necessary to first understand what emergency savings and retirement objectives are, as well as why they're both crucial. The amount of money you have set aside in a quickly accessible account to cover unforeseen expenditures, such as a job loss, medical emergency, or big home repair, is referred to as emergency savings. Retirement objectives, on the other hand, are the financial plans you put in place for when you stop working.

Both emergency savings and retirement objectives are critical, but the order in which you prioritize them will be determined by your financial position. If you have a steady income and few financial responsibilities, you may be able to focus more on your retirement objectives since you know you have a safety net in the shape of emergency funds. Yet, if you have a low income and a lot of debt, you may need to prioritize saving for emergencies to protect yourself from financial shocks.

First and foremost, save for an emergency.
These are a few reasons why emergency funds should be prioritized:

Ease of mind: Knowing that you have a safety net in place in case of an unforeseen expenditure might help you sleep easier at night.
Protects against debt: If you don't have an emergency fund, you may have to rely on credit cards or loans to pay unforeseen needs, which may rapidly lead to debt. Having an emergency fund can help you avoid falling into this trap.
Offers flexibility: Having an emergency fund in place gives you greater freedom to make financial decisions, such as taking on a new job or establishing a new business.

First and foremost, consider your retirement goals. But, there are several compelling reasons why prioritizing your retirement objectives makes sense:

The time worth of money: The sooner you begin saving for retirement, the more time your money has to grow, which can make a significant difference in the amount you have saved when you retire.

Compound interest: The strength of compound interest implies that the earlier you start saving, the less you need to save each month to achieve your goals.

Employer matching: Your company may match a percentage of your contributions if you enroll in a 401(k) or other retirement plans at work. You may dramatically enhance your retirement savings by utilizing this match.

Emergency Funds vs. Retirement Plans

So, which should take precedence? Finally, the answer will be determined by your financial condition and ambitions. In any case, striking a balance between the two is critical. You don't want to ignore your emergency funds and wind yourself in debt when an unforeseen expenditure comes, but you also don't want to ignore your retirement savings and find yourself struggling to make ends meet in your later years. Aim for three to six months of living costs in your emergency fund, and then begin contributing to your retirement objectives as soon as possible.

CHAPTER 2:

MANAGING DEBTS

What exactly is debt?
Debt is defined as something (typically money)
borrowed from one party by another. Individuals
and corporations use debt to buy purchases they
couldn't otherwise afford, and it allows them to
borrow money with the understanding that it will
be paid back at a later period. Debt agreements
typically include additional interest, which means
the borrower will end up paying back more than
they borrowed.

Interest is the fee charged by a bank or lender for
the privilege of borrowing money from them. It is
usually calculated as an annual percentage rate
(APR).

What is the issue with debt?
Debt may be an issue since it is simple to
accumulate but difficult to eliminate. The
additional interest can sometimes be so high that it
is difficult to keep up with the repayments. It's very
uncommon for payday loans to have interest rates
of +1000%, and in situations like these, many

people can hardly afford to return the interest amount and so don't wind up repaying anything off the debt sum.

This is exacerbated by the fact that it is difficult to determine the full cost of the loan before agreeing to it. Banks frequently promote 0% interest to make you feel better about taking on debt, but they don't make it obvious that this only lasts for a limited time, so after you're out of the introductory period, you'll face a significant increase in interest on whatever sum you have. There are many various types of loans available these days, so people might go into debt without even realizing it.

What kinds of debts exist?
There are many various sorts of debt, but the most prevalent include loans, credit cards, and purchase-now-pay-later schemes. In the United Kingdom, debt is classified into two types: secured debt and unsecured debt.

Secured debt refers to borrowing money against a tangible asset, most typically your home or automobile, through a mortgage or car loan. Because the lender has further security that if you are unable to repay the agreed amount, they can seize the asset and get the money back that way, interest rates on secured loans tend to be lower (meaning it is cheaper for you overall). While the low-interest rates connected with secured debt are undoubtedly advantageous, you must be assured that you can make the repayments because the implications of not paying are more severe. For example, failing to make mortgage payments might result in the loss of your home.

Personal loans, credit cards, and purchase now pay later programs are examples of unsecured debt that do not include any assets and are hence more expensive for you. This is due to the lender charging higher interest rates or fees to compensate for the increased risk. If you make a late, partial, or skipped payment, the lender is likely to charge you additional interest or fees, increasing the total amount of your debt. It may also harm your credit score, limiting your capacity to borrow money in the future.

What is APR stand for?
APR stands for Annual Percentage Rate and refers to a percentage number of how much you're going to pay in fees and interest charges when it comes to debts. For example, if you took out a £1,000 loan with a 5% APR for two years and did not make monthly payments, the total amount you would

have to return at the end of the two years would be £1,102.50.

When you sign any deal, all lenders must give you the APR amount. But, you'll often see banks market loan products with a representative APR figure attached, which signifies that at least 51% of clients will receive this rate. Nonetheless, many clients will be paid extra because it is based on their credit history. For example, if you have a terrible credit rating, the actual APR you are offered is likely to be significantly higher, leaving you with a rude surprise in the end when you realize how much you'll need to pay back.

How much debt is excessive?
Determining how much debt is too much varies from person to person since it is entirely dependent on your particular financial situation. Nonetheless, a smart place to start is to consider the amount of debt you owe in relation to your income. This is referred to as your debt-to-income ratio by financial specialists.

Divide your total monthly debt payments by your total monthly income to calculate your debt-to-income ratio. Next, to convert it to a percentage, multiply the resultant decimal by 100.

This statistic can help you determine how much of your money is going toward funding your total debt. Aim for a balance of roughly 35% or less. Anything higher than this may suggest that you have too much debt for your salary.

Another approach to knowing whether you have too much debt is to observe how you handle your money each month. If you frequently make late payments or can only make minimum payments on your credit cards, this may indicate that you have too much debt for your salary.

If you believe you have too much debt and are trying to get out of it, check out our other helpful article on how to get yourself out of debt.

Can debt ever be beneficial?
Debt is often regarded as a negative thing since it is quite expensive and may quickly become unmanageable. A little amount of debt that you can back in full each month, on the other hand, might be beneficial since it will help you create a strong credit history and a decent credit score.

It is critical to note, however, that it is not the debt itself that is beneficial. The good aspect is how you handle it. For example, if you use a credit card to cover your monthly food shopping, the sum you'll need to return will be pretty minimal, and you should have no issue paying the amount in full and on time. This demonstrates to the lender that you are a responsible borrower, which is reflected in your credit score.

Credit Score: A credit score is a three-digit rating that represents your reliability in repaying the money. That is solely based on how you have handled money in the past.

It's in your best advantage to have a good credit score because it's what a lender will use to determine whether or not to approve your loan application and at what interest rate. If you have a good credit score, you will most likely be offered lower interest rates, which means you will have to pay less interest. So, while debt isn't always a good thing, getting into manageable debt can be beneficial because it can help you get better deals in the future.

Debt Administration

People drowning in unsecured debt who have tried and failed to settle on their own or would prefer not to pursue bankruptcy may benefit from debt management.

The most significant benefit is that you may be able to reduce the amount you pay monthly toward debt obligations. If settlement proposals are accepted, you may be able to get out of debt sooner and keep more money in your pocket.

The biggest disadvantage is that creditors and lenders are not required to accept settlement offers, which could land you in court, and settling your debts will almost certainly harm your credit score. Furthermore, if the amount forgiven exceeds $600, you may owe federal income tax.

Does debt management have an impact on your credit score?
While debt management might help you get your debt under control, it can also harm your credit score.

Serious inquiries
A difficult investigation may occur at some time during debt management. For example, attempting to obtain a cheaper interest rate may result in a hard inquiry into your credit record. Hard inquiries

remain on your credit record for two years and might have a one-year impact on your credit score.

Yet, this is a short-term effect that can be quickly offset by other circumstances. For example, lowering your interest rate means you'll be able to pay your monthly bill on time, which will have a favorable impact on your payment history, which accounts for 35% of how your credit score is determined.

Payments were not made on time.
While frequent payments will improve your payment history, missed payments will severely damage your credit score. Expect your credit score to fall if you or your credit counselor use the method of withholding payment from your creditor to negotiate a lower rate.

Use of credit
Credit use is another important aspect of the health of your credit score. This element accounts for 30% of your computed score and is related to the amount of debt you have relative to your available credit. Credit usage should be between 10% and 30%. This implies that your debt should not exceed 30% of your total available credit across all accounts.

Consolidating all of your debt into a single bill will help you pay it off faster. But, closing some of your accounts will have an impact on your credit mix, which accounts for 10% of your credit score, as well as your credit history, which factors for 15%.

Additional debt-management financing methods
Choose the greatest choice for your present financial condition when deciding how to handle your debt. Debt management is one solution, but there are others to consider.

Credit cards for balance transfers
Balance transfer cards allow you to transfer your debt to a card with zero percent introductory APR. This gives you the option of paying off your debt without incurring interest. Balance transfer cards, on the other hand, have fees, including one for each balance transfer in most cases. If you do not transfer your balance to a preapproved card, your credit report may show a hard inquiry.

Debt transfer cards are accessible if your credit score is good-to-excellent, but they may not be available if your score is lower. You'll also need a solid repayment strategy in place before the zero percent interest term expires. Any residual debt will thereafter be subject to the usual variable APR.

Loans for individuals

Personal loans provide you with a single sum of money to pay off all of your debts at once. If you know you'll need extra time to bring your debt under control, a personal loan is a suitable alternative. Personal loans often have payback terms ranging from two to seven years. In contrast to a credit card, you must return your loan before the end of the set time.

Your personal loan interest rate will be determined by your credit score. Personal loan interest rates can range from 5% to 36%, so be sure the rate you obtain is lower than the rate you are now paying on your outstanding debt. Bankrate provides a tool that can predict your interest rate on some of the best personal loans available.

Is debt management appropriate for you?

Debt management can be a useful tool for debt relief, but it is not a panacea. Secured debts, such as mortgages, are not addressed by debt management. Nonetheless, it might be an option to consider if you:

Having a lot of high-interest, unsecured debt, such as credit cards.

You are approaching or have reached the maximum credit limit for each account.

Have a consistent source of money to make your payments.

Don't plan on opening a new credit account throughout your DMP.

Rather than doing it yourself, have an agency or corporation negotiate your DMP.

Overspending and other dangerous financial behaviors have been addressed.

In conclusion

Debt management may be daunting, and finding a method to get rid of it can be much more difficult. Luckily, debt management strategies such as the debt snowball, debt avalanche, DMPs, and debt settlement can assist you in obtaining the relief you want and deserve.

Yet, not all tactics are created equal, since some have greater long-term negative consequences than others. Another financing alternative, such as a balance transfer credit card or personal loan, maybe more suited. Evaluate the pros and cons of each debt management technique to make an informed selection that will help you accomplish your debt-payoff objective in the shortest amount of time while also working best for your financial circumstances.

PAYING OFF DEBTS STRATEGIES

The lender pays off all of your old obligations and rolls them into a single new loan with a single payment when you use debt consolidation. While the new interest rate may be greater than some of your other obligations, you may end up saving money by avoiding late and missing payments.

You'll need to evaluate your blended interest rate to see if it's a good plan for your scenario. It is the total interest rate paid on all of your debts. It is computed by adding up all of the interest you will pay in a year and dividing it by the total amount due. Instead, you may make use of our debt consolidation calculator.

Even though the interest rate on a debt consolidation loan is relatively high, it may be lower than the blended rate you're already paying, in which case a debt consolidation loan would be a sensible decision.

Consider debt consolidation if you can commit to not using credit cards or incurring new debt while working to pay off what you owe.

4. Debt management strategy

Nonprofit credit counseling organizations can assist debtors in developing a debt management strategy. An agency will negotiate compromises with the corporations to whom you owe money on your behalf. This might mean negotiating reduced payments, devising fair repayment arrangements, and potentially obtaining debt forgiveness.

Who this is ideal for If you struggle to make your minimum monthly payments and want a plan that will help you pay less interest and get out of debt faster, debt consolidation may be a possible choice.

Suggestions for Debt Reduction

Use these ideas to keep on track once you've established a debt repayment strategy.

1. Maintain a budget

Whichever debt-reduction approach you select, you'll need a budget. Otherwise, it's just too simple to veer off course. With a budget, you can easily see where each dollar is going, allowing you to find areas where you can cut expenditures and save money.

Whether you use an app or a spreadsheet to build a budget, after you have all of your income and spending included, you can begin preparing for debt repayment. Subtraction of fixed expenditures from income yields free cash flow. It is the amount of money you have available to cover variable costs and pay off debt.

2. Establish an emergency fund.
Nothing may derail your debt-reduction efforts like an emergency auto repair. Although you're focused on how to pay off your debt, life will continue to happen, which is why you need an emergency savings account.

Even though you wish to pay every additional dollar toward your credit card amount if you've

You'd have to charge it again if you paid off half your debt but then couldn't pay for an emergency. Most experts recommend saving three to six months' worth of living costs, so add a line item for savings when creating your budget.

3. Lower monthly expenses

Consider strategies to lower monthly costs if you're wondering how to pay off debt and save. Reducing monthly spending frees up funds that can be used to pay off debt.

Is there anything that can be cut to save money? Consider giving up Netflix or cable for a few months to save money and make time for a side venture. If your heating expenses are out of hand, several utility providers provide free energy audits that will suggest adjustments you may do to reduce utility costs.

4. Make extra money

Having a side hustle is almost as much of an American staple as apple pie. Many people now use their spare time to make jewelry to sell on Etsy, drive for a ride-sharing service, or dog-sit. The answer to the question "how can I pay off my debt?" might be to think about methods to make more money.

What are your interests? Do you have any unique abilities that you could monetize? Which side hustles would fit into your everyday routine? Discover a technique to generate extra income flow and use it toward debt repayment.

5. Investigate your debt relief alternatives.

Debt relief organizations offer lofty promises to assist with issues such as how to pay off debt, but do they deliver? Both yes and no. When you hire a debt relief firm, it negotiates with your creditors to settle or amend the conditions of your debt. Nevertheless, there is a catch.

Debt reduction firms demand fees for their services. To boost a creditor's propensity to bargain, the corporation may advise clients to cease making bill payments. However, this may result in late fees, interest charges, and other penalties, which will raise debt and harm credit ratings.

Companies can also assist in the settlement or management of some bills, but they may end up doing more harm than good. Before opting to work with one, exhaust all other possibilities.

In conclusion

There are several debt-reduction tactics and choices available. Investigate the various options, such as the debt snowball method, the debt avalanche method, and debt consolidation, to determine which one is most likely to work for you.

After you've begun, you should create a budget and an emergency savings account to make guarantee your debt doesn't spiral out of hand again.

CHAPTER 3:

INVESTING FOR THE FUTURE

Saving and investing:

Savings and investment are two distinct concepts, yet in fact, they are inextricably linked. Generally, we save first and then invest. Saving is putting money away for later use. Investment is the use of a resource (typically money) with the hope of increasing income or value growth.

Consider why saving can be crucial in your life. Putting money away for future use can help you achieve your life objectives. Saving money for emergencies, as well as short-term and long-term goals, is critical.

What happens in the event of an emergency?
Did you know that if presented with an unexpected $400 bill, 4 out of 10 individuals would either be unable to handle it or would need to borrow the money or sell something to meet the expense? Consider the possibility of an emergency in your life. Would you be able to pay for it if that

happened? If not, now is the time to devise a strategy to start saving for that emergency.

It might be difficult to imagine where you could save money at times. Begin by reviewing your spending and saving habits. Depending on your goals, you may opt to prioritize your spending differently, decrease existing costs, obtain new income, save gift money, bonuses, income tax returns, or anything else.

Develop a strategy and stick to it.
There are several strategies to save money to achieve your requirements and goals. Examples include automated savings, coin savings, and banking saves on coupons or returns. Simply consider what works best for you. One recommendation is to "pay yourself first" when you get money as a means to save money over time. When you pay yourself first, you put money aside for savings before spending it on other things.

When you've saved enough for an emergency, consider investing the rest of your savings to increase your money. Consider your immediate and long-term objectives. It is also crucial to consider your long-term savings objectives because money saved may grow over time. If you save for a long time, your savings might expand over time. Long-term savings provide advantages. Long-term savings can be invested to increase the value of your cash. Examine investing options that are suited to your goals and risk tolerance. By investing, you choose where your money will grow and give more cash to help you reach your goals.

It is never too late to start saving and investing.
Saving and investing are both key factors to consider while making long-term plans. Saving money keeps your money safe and accessible in case you need it. By investing early and consistently, your money rises in value thanks to the power of compounding.

Note that investing early, together with compound interest, might result in larger investment amounts than investing later. Take the time to consider your current and future financial requirements and objectives.

INVESTMENT IS IMPORTANT

Hardly everyone saves for retirement, and even those who do may not be saving enough to carry them through their golden years. According to a

2020 Federal Reserve research, around 25% of non-retirees were not saving for retirement. Everyone, however, needs to invest to build wealth, combat inflation, and save for retirement and other financial goals.

Investing does not have to entail big quantities of money saved. Compound interest allows you to make money on your initial investment plus any collected interest from prior periods. While everyone should invest, everyone's investment approach is unique to their personal and financial goals.

To begin investing, you do not need a large sum of money. Because of the power of compounding, even tiny sums of your money may yield more money quickly.

Investing may help you build wealth, achieve financial objectives, outperform inflation, and save for retirement.

One investing approach does not suit all investors. Your financial references will be distinct from those of your friends and relatives.

Your investing plan is determined by your financial status, the amount of risk you are prepared to accept, the length of time you want to invest, and other considerations.

What Exactly Is Investing?

The act of acquiring assets or things to create income and gain is known as investing. Investments, which are acquired assets or things, are utilized to generate future prosperity. These items are frequently in the form of stocks or bonds, but they may also include real estate or other assets like cryptocurrencies or gold.

Why Should You Make an Investment?

Investing your money is essential for several reasons. You want to build wealth to aid you in times of need, if you lose your career, or for future aspirations. You should also take advantage of compounding while accounting for inflation so that your money does not lose value over time. Furthermore, if you intend to quit working and retire at some time, investment is critical to achieving those objectives.

Let's look at some of the reasons why investment is vital.

Creating Wealth

To various people, wealth might imply different things. It might be characterized as a certain quantity of money in your bank account or as financial objectives you establish for yourself. Investing can help you get there in any case.

If you want to pay off debt, send your child to college, purchase a house, start a company, or save for retirement, investment can help you get there faster than cash in your bank account. You may develop wealth via investing, which is the rise in the value of all of your assets.

Money creation is more than simply a goal that will aid you throughout your life. Building generational wealth through investment allows you to leave a financial legacy. Generational wealth can not only offer a solid financial foundation for your children, but it can also help to close the wealth gap that many communities suffer.

Compounding
Compound interest may be used to your advantage while investing. Compound interest is the interest gained on your invested funds plus the interest earned in previous periods. It is also known as "interest on interest." Compound interest helps you to rapidly increase your money. For instance, if you contributed $50 every month for 15 years, your total contribution would be $9,000. Assuming a 10% rate of return, that $9,000 would have grown

to more than $19,000 in that time due to compound interest.

To Combat Inflation
Inflation is defined as the total increase in product prices over time. If prices rise over time, your money will purchase less today than it did yesterday. If there is inflation over a 30- or 40-year period, your money will be worth much less while the cost of living has risen. Investing your money is one method to combat inflation. If your money earns more than the rate of inflation, it will be worth more tomorrow than it is today.

Retirement
If you intend to quit working and retire, you must have a substantial amount of money saved to live on after you no longer work. Investing can help you close the gap between what you save and what you need to live on for the next 20 or 30 years.

To begin investing for retirement, work backward from a retirement savings goal you've set for yourself. That figure can be determined by considering how soon you want to retire and what kind of lifestyle and expenses you anticipate having in retirement. You can then devise a retirement investing strategy that aligns your current financial situation with your retirement objectives.

How Much Money Should You Put Into It?
While you can invest for short-term goals such as home ownership, most people invest for retirement. People in the United States typically choose to retire around the age of 65 if they are financially able to do so. This means that they will have to rely on their investments to fund their lifestyle for the rest of their lives. In retirement, there are still expenses to be paid, such as utilities, housing, food, and travel.

Financial experts recommend a few different methods for determining how much you should invest now to fund retirement or other goals.

These rules or formulas may not apply to everyone. When determining how much and how to invest your money, consider your financial status.

Save aside 20% of your pay.
Some gurus recommend saving 20% of your earnings. It implies you may live on 80% of your salary for housing, needs, and desires. Many people choose this strategy since it is simple to set away a part of their money each payday. Most of the time,

you may automate 20% of your salary to go directly into an investment account each month, making this one of the most advantageous techniques to utilize. It, however, may not be achievable for everyone.

The 4% Principle
The 4% rule is another rule of thumb that many financial professionals employ. It implies that taking 4% of your retirement assets each year will provide you with enough money to live on while still earning enough returns to preserve its current worth after adjusting for inflation. For example, if you had $1.25 million in retirement savings, you might take $50,000 in the first year under the 4% rule. The next year, you should be able to take another 4% of the remaining amount, and the cycle should repeat itself for the duration of your retirement.

This approach is important because if you can estimate your yearly retirement costs, you can work backward from that number to establish how much money you need to save each month until retirement.

A single investment strategy does not work for everyone.

Your investing plan is unique to you and should be based on your objectives and risk tolerance. You could have some short-term objectives, such as buying a vehicle or a house, as well as some long-term ones, such as saving for retirement. Knowing your unique risk tolerance is vital since various people can stomach significant swings in the value of their assets, whilst others become quite worried if the value of an investment lowers.

Investments frequently recover in the long run. As of March 2022, the S&P 500, one of the most widely followed stock indices, has returned an average of 12% over the previous ten years.

If you are afraid of risk, your investing strategy will be shaped toward more diversified or even short-term assets. Longer-term investments may be riskier in some assets since there is greater uncertainty over a longer time horizon; yet, longer investment periods may help average out periods of outsized short-term profits or losses in other assets.

There is a risk-reward trade-off in investment, which indicates that when an asset has a higher risk, it tends to provide a larger payoff.

It may take some time to develop your investment plan, and most investors adjust their methods as their living circumstances change. Those who are younger, for example, are riskier in their investments, but elderly individuals are less risky since they have fewer working years to recoup any financial losses.

Closing the Wealth Divide
Investment may also assist people and communities that frequently find the deck stacked against them in terms of financial prospects owing to the wealth divide.

Women, for example, would normally need to spend more and for a longer length of time to reach retirement aspirations, because they are frequently paid less than their male colleagues for the same profession and have a seven-year longer average global lifetime.

3 Despite evidence indicating that women are stronger investors than males, they tend to be more conservative in their investments, therefore adopting a more proactive and aggressive strategy may benefit women.

People in Black or Hispanic populations are recognized to have fewer resources and wealth, which is aggravated by the racial wealth gap widening. According to the 2019 Survey of Consumer Finances, Black families had 7.8 times less median household wealth than White households, and Hispanic households had 5.2 times less median household wealth. 6 Investment might be a modest step toward closing the wealth divide.

INVESTMENT TYPES AND THEIR RISKS AND REWARDS

Many individuals are intimidated by investing since there are so many possibilities and it may be difficult to determine which assets are best for your account. This tutorial will lead you through 10 of the most common forms of investments, from stocks to commodities, and explain why you should include them in your portfolio. If you're serious about investing, it can make sense to seek the advice of a financial adviser who can guide you and help you choose which assets will help you achieve your objectives.

1. Securities

Stocks, often known as shares or equities, are perhaps the most well-known and straightforward sort of investing. When you buy stock, you are purchasing a share in a publicly listed corporation. Several of the country's largest corporations are publicly listed, which means you may acquire shares in them. Exxon, Apple, and Microsoft are a few examples.

How to Make Money: When you acquire a stock, you hope that the price will rise so that you may sell it for a profit. The danger, of course, is that the stock price may fall, causing you to lose money.

2. Bonds
When you purchase a bond, you are effectively lending money to a company. In most cases, this is a company or a government agency. Corporations issue corporate bonds, whereas municipalities issue municipal bonds. The United States Treasury issues Treasury bonds, notes, and bills, which are all debt securities that investors purchase.

How to Make Money: The lender or investor receives interest payments while the money is being loaned. You get your principal back when the bond matures, which means you've kept it for the contractually specified period.

Bonds normally provide a lower rate of return than stocks, but they also carry a smaller risk. Of course, there is still some danger involved. The corporation from which you purchase a bond may fail, or the government may default. Government bonds, notes, and bills, on the other hand, are regarded as extremely secure investments.

3. Investing in Mutual Funds

A mutual fund is a collection of money from numerous investors that is invested extensively in a variety of firms. Mutual funds can be managed actively or passively. An actively managed fund has a fund manager who chooses which securities to invest clients' money in. Fund managers frequently attempt to outperform a certain market index by selecting investments that outperform the index. An index fund, often known as a passively managed fund, merely tracks a major stock markets index such as the Dow Jones Industrial Average or the S& P 500. Mutual funds can invest in a diverse range of securities, including stocks, bonds, commodities, currencies, and derivatives.

Mutual funds, depending on their investments, entail many of the same dangers as stocks and bonds. Nonetheless, the risk is frequently lower since the assets are automatically diversified.

Investors profit from mutual funds when the value of the stocks, bonds, and other packaged assets in which the fund invests rises. You can purchase them directly from the management firm or via discount brokerages. Nevertheless, there is usually a minimum investment and an annual charge.

4. ETFs (Exchange-Traded Funds) (ETFs)
ETFs are similar to mutual funds in that they are a group of investments that track a market index. Unlike mutual funds, which are acquired through a fund firm, ETF shares are traded on stock exchanges. Its price varies during the trading day, but the value of mutual funds is simply the net asset value of your assets, which is computed at the end of each trading session.

How to Profit: ETFs profit from the accumulation of a return across all of their investments. Because ETFs are more diversified than individual equities, they are frequently advised to begin investors. You may reduce risk even further by investing in an ETF that tracks a wide index. Moreover, like mutual funds, you may profit from an ETF by selling it when its value rises.

5. Certificate of Deposit (CDs)

Investment experts view certificates of deposit (CDs) as very low-risk options. You lend money to a bank for a predetermined time, and you get interested in that money. You receive your principal back along with the predetermined amount of interest after that period has passed. Your interest rate is probably going to be higher the longer the loan term. The potential return is low, but the risk is also low.

How to profit: With a CD, you profit from the interest you earn throughout the deposit. For long-term financial savings, CDs are a solid choice. They are FDIC-insured up to $250,000, which would protect your funds even if your bank were to fail, so there are no significant dangers. Nonetheless, you must be certain that you won't use the funds during the CD's term because early withdrawals are subject to severe penalties.

6. Investing Types and Retirement Plans

An investment account with specific tax advantages where participants place their money for retirement is known as a retirement plan. Retirement plans come in many different forms, including workplace retirement plans offered by your company, such as 401(k) and 403(b) plans. If your company does not provide a retirement plan, you may be able to open an individual retirement account (IRA) or a Roth IRA.

Retirement plans aren't a distinct class of investments per se, but rather a method to purchase stocks, bonds, and funds in two tax-advantaged ways. The first one allows you to invest pretax money (as with a traditional IRA). The second one lets you withdraw money without having to pay taxes on it. The investments' risks are the same as if you had purchased them outside of a retirement plan.

7. Choices
An option is a little more sophisticated or intricate means to purchase shares. You purchase the right to buy or sell an asset at a specific price and at a specific time when you purchase an option. Options come in two flavors: call options, which are used to purchase assets, and put options, which are used to sell options.

How to make money: As an investor, you fix the price of a stock with the anticipation that its value will increase. The stock might potentially lose money, which is the risk associated with an option. So, you lose the money from the contract if the stock's price falls from when it was first purchased. Options are a sophisticated investment strategy, thus individual investors should use caution while employing them.

8. Pensions

When you acquire an annuity, you do it in exchange for a policy of insurance and regular payments. These payments typically start in retirement, but they are sometimes made years in advance. Because of this, a lot of people use annuities in their retirement savings strategy.

There are several different types of annuities. They could exist forever or only for a certain amount of time. They could ask for a single upfront payment or recurring premium payments. They might have a loose connection to the stock market or they could just be an insurance policy without any connection to the markets. Payments can be made right now or put off until a certain time. They might be constant or changeable.

How to make money: Annuities can ensure an additional source of retirement income. They aren't high-growth, but they are relatively low-risk.

Investors usually treat them as a good addition to their retirement savings as opposed to a primary source of funding.

9. Derivatives:
A financial instrument known as a derivative derives its value from another asset. It is a two-party contract that is comparable to an annuity. However, in this instance, the contract is a commitment to sell an asset at a specified price in the future. The investor is placing a wager that the value won't fall if they choose to buy the derivative. Institutional investors typically buy derivatives because they are thought of as more sophisticated investments.

The following are the top three categories of derivatives:

Options Contracts: An option allows the investor the chance to purchase or sell a certain asset at a particular price at a particular point in the future. You have the choice to sell the asset at that price with a put option and to acquire it at that price with a call option.
Contracts for future sales: A future contract guarantees that a sale will be made at a specific time and on a specific date.

Swaps: This is an arrangement for two parties to trade future cash flows.

Ways to generate income: If you are on the right side of price changes, investing in derivatives may be profitable. For instance, if you promise to buy copper for $1,000 in nine months but the market price is $2,000 at that point, your investment has virtually quadrupled.

10. Materials

Physical goods that you may invest in are known as commodities. They are widespread in futures markets where producers and commercial purchasers, or experts, try to protect their financial interest in the commodities.

Before investing in futures, retail investors should make sure they fully understand them. That's in part because investing in commodities entails a risk that unexpected developments might cause a commodity's price to change suddenly and abruptly in either way. Political decisions, for example, may significantly alter the price of something like oil, whilst the weather might affect the price of agricultural items.

The four major categories of commodities are broken down as follows:

Metals: industrial metals and precious metals (such as gold and silver) (copper)

Crops: wheat, corn, and soybeans

Livestock includes feeding cattle and pork pies.

Energy comes from crude oil, petroleum, and natural gas.

Ways to generate income: Trading commodity futures is the main way that investors profit from commodities. Commodities are occasionally purchased by investors to use as an inflation hedge for their portfolios. Via equities, mutual funds, exchange-traded funds (ETFs), and futures contracts, you may acquire commodities indirectly.

How to Purchase Various Assets

You may buy the many kinds of assets you might be interested in buying in one of two methods, but you must have an open investing account in both cases. Both are simple to execute, but only one offers a service that is finished for you. The two main strategies to purchase the kinds of assets you desire are as follows:

Open a Brokerage Account Online: If you decide to handle your investments, you may do so by opening a brokerage account. With the opportunity to purchase stocks, bonds, mutual funds, and more in a matter of minutes, this enables you to start going immediately. The fact that you will be making all final financial decisions by yourself is the only drawback.

Hire a Financial Advisor: Hiring a financial advisor is another option for purchasing various investment types. The advisor can help you develop a comprehensive financial plan and adequately get ready for retirement in addition to giving you access to buy and trade assets. In that you only need to approve trades or investments, the advisor takes care of the details, making this more of an automated process. If you need assistance, your advisor can help you open a brokerage account.

Conclusion

There are many different investment options available. Some are ideal for beginners, while others call for more knowledge and investigation. No matter what your objective may be, there are a few good options available to you because each type of investment has a different level of risk and reward. Before choosing an asset allocation that is in line with their overall financial objectives, investors should take into account each type of investment.

STRATEGIES FOR INVESTING FOR THE LONG-TERM

Investing is one of the greatest methods to safeguard your financial future, and one of the best ways to invest is over an extended period. Throughout the previous several years, it would have been tempting to stray from a long-term strategy and go after rapid gains. So it's more crucial than ever to concentrate on long-term investment while according to your strategy.

Today's investors have a variety of options for where to put their money and may decide how much risk they're ready to accept to suit their needs. You can choose extremely secure assets, like a certificate of deposit (CD), or you can increase the risk and possible reward by choosing investments like equities, mutual funds, or ETFs.

Equities are Americans' second-most preferred long-term investment behind real estate. The following list notably includes both categories.
Instead, you may try a little bit of everything, diversifying your portfolio so that it has a good chance of succeeding in virtually any market.

1. Stocks in growth

Growth stocks are the Ferraris of the stock market. High growth and excellent investment returns are what they claim. Tech businesses are frequently growth stocks, although this is not a must.

Companies rarely pay out a dividend, at least not until their growth slows down since they typically reinvest all of their profits back into the company.

Who are they excellent for?: If you plan to purchase individual growth stocks, you need properly research the business, which can take a lot of time.
You'll also need to have a high-risk tolerance or make a commitment to owning the stocks for at least three to five years due to the volatility of growth stocks.

Risks: Growth stocks are prone to risk because investors sometimes overpay for the stock in comparison to the company's profitability.

So, these stocks may lose a significant amount of value very fast in the event of a bad market or recession. It looks as though their unexpected fame vanishes in a moment. But, over time, growth stocks have been among the greatest performers.

Rewards: If you can identify the perfect firm, the prize might be endless because the two largest corporations in the world, Google and Amazon, have seen rapid development.

Where to buy them: Any online broker that provides stock trading is a good place to buy them.

2. Stock funds
Overview: A stock fund is a collection of equities, sometimes tied together by a common theme or classification, such as big or American stocks. With this product, the fund firm levies a fee, but it may be quite little.

Who are they ideal for? A stock fund, such as an ETF or a mutual fund, might be a wonderful alternative if you're not yet ready to invest the time and effort in evaluating individual stocks.
If an investor wants to use stocks more aggressively but lacks the time or motivation to make investments their full-time pastime, a stock fund is a great option.

Risks: Investing in a stock fund is less effort and less hazardous than buying individual stocks.
Nonetheless, it may still change significantly from year to year, sometimes losing as much as 30% or

even gaining 30% in some of its most dramatic years.

Be mindful that your fund will be less diversified than one based on a broad index like the S&P 500 if you purchase a fund that isn't widely diversified, such as one centered on one sector. Thus if you invested in a fund that depends on the chemical sector, the price of oil may have a significant impact on it. Several of the stocks in the portfolio might likely suffer if oil prices increase.

Rewards: Because a stock fund owns more companies—and not all of them are going to succeed in any one year—your returns should be more steady. A stock fund will be easier to hold and manage than individual equities. You will also have a lot of potential gains with a stock fund. The top index funds are shown below.

Several high-growth equities will be included in a broadly diversified fund that you purchase, such as an S&P 500 index fund or a Nasdaq-100 index fund, in addition to many others. But, you'll possess a more diverse and secure group of businesses than if you only owned a few individual stocks.

A stock fund will often be less volatile than holding only a few individual stocks since you will receive the weighted average return of all the firms in the portfolio.

Where to buy them: Virtually any online broker that sells mutual funds and ETFs is where you may buy them.

3. Bond funds

A bond fund, whether it be a mutual fund or an exchange-traded fund (ETF), includes several bonds from many issuers. A bond fund's kind, length, risk level, issuer (corporate, local government, or federal government), and other variables are often used to describe it.

When a business or the government issues a bond, it promises to give the bond's owner a predetermined yearly interest payment. The issuer pays back the bond's principal at the end of its term, and the bond is then redeemed.

Who are they useful for? Investors who want a diversified portfolio of bonds without having to research and purchase individual bonds can consider bond funds.

Furthermore, as bond ETFs are sometimes available for less than $100, they are advantageous for individual investors who lack the funds necessary to acquire a single bond, which typically costs approximately $1,000.

Risks: Although bonds can change, a bond fund will be comparatively stable, moving only in reaction to changes in the current interest rate.
Compared to stocks, bonds are thought to be safer, but not all issuers are created equal.

Government issuers, particularly the federal government, are seen as being fairly safe, whereas business issuers might be anything between somewhat less and much riskier.

Rewards: Bonds may be among the safer investments, and when they are part of a fund, they become even safer. A fund diversifies its assets and lowers the effect of any one bond failing on the portfolio because it may own hundreds of various bond kinds from several different issuers.

Typically, the return on a bond or bond fund is substantially lower than it would be on a stock fund; it may be 4 to 5 percent yearly, but it is often lower on government bonds. It carries a lot less dangerous as well.

There are several bond fund options available to suit your needs if you're seeking one.

Where to buy them: Virtually every online broker that sells mutual funds and ETFs also has bond funds that you may invest in.

4. Income stocks

Overview: Dividend stocks can provide respectable returns but are less likely to soar higher as quickly as growth equities, which are the sports cars of the stock market.

A stock that pays a dividend, or a regular cash distribution, is just one that does that. Many equities pay dividends, but they tend to belong to more established, older businesses that don't need as much cash.

Older investors like dividend stocks because they provide a consistent income and the finest firms raise that dividend over time, allowing you to earn more than you would with a bond's set distribution. One well-liked type of dividend stock is REITs.

Who are they suitable for? Dividend stocks are best for long-term buy-and-hold investors, especially those who want or require a cash distribution and desire less volatility than the market average.

Risks: Although dividend stocks are often less volatile than growth stocks, don't assume they won't have substantial ups and downs, particularly if the stock market experiences a difficult period.

Yet, a dividend-paying corporation is often safer than a growth company since it is more established and mature.

But, if a dividend-paying firm doesn't make enough money to cover its dividend, it will reduce the payout, which might cause its price to fall.

Rewards: A dividend stock's payment is one of its main selling points, and some of the best firms offer payouts of up to 4% yearly. But more crucially, they can increase payments by 8 or 10 percent annually over extended periods, meaning you'll get paid more normally every year.

Although there is a chance for significant gains, they won't typically be as high as with growth companies. Moreover, there are several dividend stock funds accessible if you wish to invest in them to hold a diverse range of stocks.

Where to buy them: Any online broker that provides stock trading is a good place to buy them.

5. Value stocks
Overview: Many stocks have stretched valuations during periods of significant market gains. When that occurs, a lot of investors look to value stocks as a means to be more protective while still having a chance to make good profits.

Value stocks are less expensive based on valuation criteria like a price-earnings ratio, which calculates how much investors are paying for every dollar of earnings.
Growth stocks, which often expand quicker and have greater values, are compared with value stocks.

Who are they excellent for? Value stocks may be a tempting choice given their propensity to perform well during periods of increasing interest rates. Also, the Federal Reserve has recently started hiking interest rates at a rapid pace.

Risks: Value stocks frequently have less potential for loss, therefore they typically decline less when the market does. They can still increase if the market does, too.

Rewards: If the market once again supports value stocks, their values may grow more quickly than those of other non-value equities. Since you may earn above-average returns while assuming less risk, value stocks are appealing.
Several value stocks also pay dividends, so you may potentially earn some extra money there.

Where to buy them: Any online broker that provides stock trading is a good place to buy them.

6 . Target-date investments
Overview: If you don't want to manage your portfolio, target-date funds are a wonderful choice. As you become older, these funds grow more conservative, making your portfolio safer as you go closer to retirement and will need the money. When your goal date draws closer, these funds gradually switch your assets from riskier equities to safer bonds.

where to purchase them Although you may purchase target-date funds outside of 401(k) plans, they are a popular option in many employment plans. The fund handles the remainder when you choose your retirement year.

Risk: As target-date funds are just a mix of stock funds and bond funds, they will generally have many of the same risks as both. Your fund will possess a bigger percentage of equities if your target date is decades away, which means it will be more volatile at the beginning. The fund will move more toward bonds as your goal date approaches, resulting in less fluctuation but lower earnings.
A target-date fund will often begin to underperform the stock market by a rising margin since it steadily shifts toward more bonds over time. Return is being given up for safety.

Benefits: Some financial planners advise buying a target-date fund five or 10 years beyond the actual date you expect to retire so that you'll enjoy the additional gain from equities. This reduces the chance of outliving your money. Your results are ultimately determined by the investments made by the fund. A better long-term return should result from more stock, but a lower long-term return should result from more bonds.

Where to buy them: Virtually any online broker that sells mutual funds and ETFs is where you may buy them.

7. Real estate
Starting costs a lot of money, fees are exorbitant, and profits are frequently obtained by owning an asset for a longer period rather than just a few years.

Real estate investing may be an appealing option, in part because you can borrow money from the bank for the majority of the investment and pay it back gradually.

Who are they beneficial for? Owning a property provides people the chance to be their boss, and various tax regulations favor property owners in particular.
Nonetheless, even though real estate is sometimes seen as a passive investment, renting out the home may require much active management on your part.

Risks: When you borrow a sizable sum of money, you increase the likelihood that your investment may fail. Yet, even if you pay cash for real estate, you'll still have a lot of money invested in just one thing, and a lack of diversification might lead to issues if the asset is damaged.

Moreover, even if the home is vacant, you will still be responsible for covering the mortgage and other maintenance expenses out of your own money.

Rewards: Although there are potential high dangers, there are also potential big benefits. If you choose a nice property and take good care of it, if you're prepared to stay on the asset for a while, you can make several times your initial investment.

Also, if you pay off the mortgage on a house, you may benefit from more stability and income flow, which attracts elderly investors to rental property. Here are some suggestions for purchasing a rental property.

Where to find them: A licensed real estate broker can be used to purchase the property.

8. Small-cap stocks
Overview: Small-cap stocks, or the shares of very tiny firms, are popular among investors because of their ability to develop swiftly or eventually take advantage of an emerging market. In actuality, the retail behemoth Amazon began as a small-cap

stock, and holders of the shares became quite wealthy.

Usually, but not usually, small-cap stocks are also high-growth stocks.

Who are they good for?: Purchasing individual stocks requires extensive research and analysis, but small-caps can be a great place to find the stocks that other investors have overlooked.
However, these start-up businesses are typically much more volatile than more well-known, larger companies, so investors need to have a steel stomach.

Risks: Small-cap stocks often have higher risks than high-growth firms. Because they have fewer financial resources, fewer accesses to capital markets, and less clout in their marketplaces, small businesses are just more hazardous overall (less brand recognition, for example).

Similar to growth companies, investors will frequently pay a high price for a small-cap stock's earnings, particularly if it has the potential to expand or become a dominant business in the future. Also, small-cap companies may see a sharp decline during a difficult period in the market due to their high price tag.

Small-cap firms are notoriously unstable, and their stock prices can change drastically from year to year. In addition to the price fluctuation, the company is often smaller and has fewer financial resources than a bigger one. Small-cap companies are therefore thought to have higher business risk than medium- and large-sized firms.

It takes time and effort to evaluate individual firms, which is a need if you plan to acquire them. So, not everyone should invest in small businesses. (You might also want to take into account a few of the top small-cap ETFs.)

Rewards: Finding a good small-cap company may yield 20 percent annual returns or more for decades, especially if you can purchase a truly hidden gem like Amazon before anybody realizes just how great it could eventually turn out to be.

Where to buy them: Any online broker that provides stock trading is a good place to buy them.

9. Robo-advisor portfolio:

Overview: A robo-advisor portfolio is automatically invested depending on your goals, time horizon, and risk tolerance when you deposit money into the robo account. Before managing the entire process, the robo-advisor will ask you a few questions to help it understand what you need from the service. Your portfolio will be built by the robo-advisor, who will choose investments, often low-cost ETFs.

What does the service cost you? a robo-advisor's management fee, which is typically approximately 0.25 percent yearly, plus the cost of any funds in the account. The cost of investment funds varies depending on how much money you invest with them, but funds in robo accounts normally cost between 0.06 percent and 0.15 percent, or $6 and $15 for every $10,000 invested.

A robo-advisor can, at its best, create for you an investment portfolio that is well-diversified and can accommodate your long-term demands.
Who are they useful to? If you don't want to do any investing yourself and would rather leave it to an expert, robo-advisors are a fantastic option.

You may arrange the account with a robo-advisor to be as aggressive or cautious as you'd like. You can choose that path if you desire all stocks at all times.

Two of the top robo-advisors, Wealthfront and Betterment, provide the option for the account to be primarily in cash or a basic savings account.

Risks: A robo-advisor's heavily influenced by your investments. You can anticipate greater volatility if you invest heavily in stock funds due to your high-risk tolerance than if you buy bonds or keep cash in a savings account. So, the risk is in your possessions.

Rewards: The potential return on a robo-advisor account also varies depending on the investments and may be very high if you own largely stock funds or low if you keep safer assets like cash in a high-yield savings account.

A robo-advisor will frequently create a diversified portfolio so that you have a more consistent stream of yearly returns, but doing so will result in a somewhat lower total return.

Where to obtain them: Some robo-advisors allow you to establish an account. These are the top robo-advisors available today.

10. Roth IRA:

Overview: A Roth IRA may be the greatest retirement plan available. It enables you to save after taxes, let your money grow tax-free over a long period, and then extract it tax-free. Also, you may avoid paying taxes on the transfer of that money to your heirs, making it a more desirable option than a standard IRA.

Who are they excellent for? Anybody earning an income can use a Roth IRA to accumulate tax-free assets for retirement.

Risks: A Roth IRA is more of a shell for your account with particular tax and legal advantages than an actual investment. You may invest in nearly anything that suits your needs if you have an account at one of the finest brokerages for Roth IRAs.

An IRA CD is a smart choice if you are risk-averse and want a guaranteed income with no potential for loss. A CD is all that is invested in this IRA.

Also, as long as you follow the plan's guidelines, you won't pay taxes on the interest you earn inside a tax-friendly IRA.

When the CD matures, there is nearly no chance that you won't get your dividend and your principal back. It's near as risk-free an investment as there is, but inflation is still something to be aware of.

Benefits: You may invest in stocks and stock funds to possibly earn considerably bigger returns and do it tax-free if you want to take things up a notch.

Of course, you'll have to put up with the additional dangers that stock and stock fund investment entails.

You can open an account at a brokerage or robo-advisor to obtain them. The top brokerages for Roth IRAs at this time are listed below.

The fundamentals of long-term investment
The route to a secure future may be through long-term investing. So it's crucial to have these guidelines in mind as you proceed.

Know the dangers associated with your investing.
In investment, taking on greater risk typically results in a better return. As a result, relatively secure investments like CDs often have low rates, while bonds and other medium-risk assets like high-yield equities have slightly higher yields.

Investors that seek a bigger return typically have to assume greater risk.

Although stocks have historically performed well overall—the Standard & Poor's 500 indexes have returned 10% over lengthy periods—stocks are notorious for their volatility. A stock's price might fluctuate by 50% in a single year, either up or down. Best short-term investments can be a lot safer.

Choose a plan that you can stick to.
Can you endure a greater degree of danger in exchange for a greater reward? Knowing your risk tolerance and if you worry when your assets lose value is crucial. If an investment still can increase, you must do everything in your power to resist selling it when it is down. Selling an investment only to see it increase even further after you've done so might be discouraging.

Make sure you comprehend your investment plan so that you have a greater chance of maintaining it when it becomes unpopular. While no investment strategy is successful 100% of the time, it's important to keep an eye on the big picture and adhere to your game plan.

Understand your time frame.

By committing to keep your investments for a longer period, you can reduce your risk. You will have more time to weather the market's ups and downs thanks to the extended holding period.

The S&P 500 index has a strong track record, but those returns were compounded over time, so the index might decline significantly in a short amount of time. So, investors should be able to maintain their money in the market for at least three to five years, and the longer the better. Short-term investments, like high-yield savings accounts, maybe a better choice if you are unable to accomplish that.

As a result, time may be a powerful ally in your investment. You don't have to spend all of your time monitoring your assets and worrying about short-term movements, which is beneficial for those who commit to investing in the long run. A long-term strategy can be established and then put (largely) on autopilot.

Make careful to diversify your holdings.
As was previously said, no investing plan is always successful. Because of this, investors must diversify their portfolios.

Index funds are a fantastic, inexpensive approach to quickly gain diversity. You may invest in a big number of businesses that are categorized according to factors like size or location. You may quickly assemble a diverse portfolio by holding a handful of these types of funds.

While investing all of your funds in one or two stocks could sound thrilling, a diversified portfolio will carry less risk and should still generate positive returns over time.

Is now the right moment to invest in equities for the long term?
It's virtually always a good time to invest if you have a long-term outlook on the stock market and are appropriately diversifying your portfolio. This is so because, as the adage goes, time in the market is more essential than timing the market since the market tends to rise with time.

During the long haul, the market (as represented by the Standard & Poor's 500 indexes) has increased by around 10% annually. More of that return is likely to be yours if you invest for a longer period.

But, that does not imply that you should immediately invest all of your money in the market.

Soon, there is a lot of room for movement. It is better to make frequent investments, such as once a week or once a month, and to continue to do so over time. You'll make use of the dollar-cost averaging technique to avoid paying an excessive amount when you buy.

This method of contributing money with each paycheck is something you already do, for example, if you routinely contribute to your employer's 401(k) account. Long-term investment benefits from regularity and investing discipline of this caliber.

Long-term investing may be beneficial at any time, but it can be particularly profitable when stock prices have already declined significantly, like during recessions. Falling stock prices provide a chance to purchase equities at a discount, which may result in better long-term profits. Unfortunately, many investors become too hesitant to buy and profit when equities fall significantly.

Another benefit of investing consistently during good times and bad is that you'll be able to keep increasing your investment even when the price is low, maybe finding a great deal. Yet, it implies that you must prepare in advance and have your brokerage account opened and financed.

Why are long-term investments a wise choice?
You have the chance to earn more money with long-term investments than you can with short-term ones. The caveat is that you must have a long-term outlook and resist the urge to leave the market because your investment has lost value or because you want to sell now to make a fast profit.

You'll be able to escape the short-term noise that leads many investors astray by committing to the long-term and not selling your investments when the market declines. For instance, investors in the S&P 500 who hung on after the precipitous decline in early 2020 were probably able to endure the immediate hiccups brought on by the beginning of the COVID epidemic before markets recovered and raced upward once more.

In addition, investing for the long term frees you from the constant market attention required by short-term traders. Instead of worrying about the market's movements, you may invest your money on autopilot regularly and spend your time doing activities you truly like.

One of the best strategies to amass wealth over time is to invest for the long term. Yet the first step is to develop long-term thinking skills and stop excessively tracking the daily ups and downs of the market.

CHAPTER 4:

BUILDING YOUR BUSINESS

You must adjust to shifting circumstances if you want to manage a successful firm.

Making a business strategy requires doing extensive market research on your industry and the characteristics of your target market. Conducting surveys, hosting focus groups, and looking into SEO and public statistics are all part of this.

You need to establish your brand and gain a following of customers that are interested in what your business has to offer in addition to selling your product or service.

This article is for company owners who wish to understand the fundamental procedures for launching a new enterprise.

Establishing a business can be challenging, but if you divide the procedure into manageable parts, you can make it simpler. Use this 10-step checklist to turn your business from an idea in your brain into a genuine thing rather than wasting time guessing where to begin and spinning your wheels.

BUSINESS STARTING TECHNIQUES
1. Clarify your concept, your business concept.

You most certainly already have a concept of what you want to offer online, or at the very least, the market you want to join, if you're thinking about launching a business. Look up current businesses in the industry you've chosen. See how you can improve what you're doing by studying what the current market leaders are doing. You have a good concept and are prepared to write a business plan if you believe your company can offer something that other businesses can't (or can do the same thing, but more quickly and cheaply).

What is your "why"?
Glenn Gutek, CEO of Awake Consulting and Coaching, advised Business News Daily to "always start with why." "It's important to understand why you're starting your business. It may be prudent to distinguish between the business's service in a personal way and a market why throughout this procedure. The scope of your business will always be greater than one that is created to address a personal need if your why is centered on filling a need in the market.

Think about franchising.
Opening a franchise of an established business is an additional choice. You just need a decent site and

the money to support your firm; the concept, brand recognition, and business plan are already in place.

Name-drop ideas for your company.
Whatever solution you select, it's critical to comprehend the justification for your notion. Owner of Business by Design and former director of operations and women's business programs at Covation Center Stephanie Desaulniers advises company owners against creating a business plan or coming up with a name before determining the idea's viability.

Searching for small business financing, please? To have our vendor partners get in touch with you regarding your needs, please fill out the form below.

Specify who your target market is.
Desaulniers claimed that individuals begin their businesses much too frequently without first taking the time to consider their target market and the reasons why they would want to buy from or hire them.

You need to be more specific about why you want to work with these clients; are you passionate about making people's lives easier? stated Desaulniers. Or delight in producing art to enliven their surroundings? Finding these solutions clarifies your objective. Thirdly, decide how you will offer this value to your clients and how to convey it so they will be eager to pay for it.

You must work out the essential details at the brainstorming stage. It could be time to come up with alternative ideas if the concept doesn't excite you or if there isn't a market for it.

Determine your "why," your target market and the name of your company to improve your business concept.

2. Create a business strategy

When your concept is ready, you must ask yourself a few crucial questions: What is the goal of your company? To whom are you marketing? What are you trying to achieve? How will you pay for the first costs? A strong company strategy can provide answers to these queries.

By jumping into things without thinking them through, inexperienced business entrepreneurs might make a lot of blunders. You must identify your ideal clientele. Who will purchase your good or service? If you can't uncover any indication that there is a market for your concept, what would be the point?

run a market analysis.
Making a business strategy requires doing extensive market research on your industry and the characteristics of your target market. Focus groups, polls, and studies on SEO and open data are all part of this process.

You may better understand your industry, rivals, and your target client by conducting market research to learn more about their requirements, preferences, and behavior. To better understand the potential and constraints in your industry, many small company experts advise obtaining demographic data and performing a competition study.

The finest small businesses set themselves out from the competition with unique goods or services. This has a big influence on your competitive environment and enables you to offer potential clients distinct value.
Consider an exit strategy.
While you put together your company plan, it's also a good idea to think about an exit strategy. Making

a rough plan for how you'll eventually leave the company pushes you to think forward.

According to Josh Tolley, "young entrepreneurs are too frequently so enthusiastic about their firm and so certain that everyone will be a customer that they spend very little if any, time to explain the plan on exiting the business."

"What do they show you initially when you get on an airplane? How to escape from it. What are the things they highlight before the film starts when you go to the movies? locations of the exits. They line up all the children during your first week of kindergarten and instruct them on fire drills to leave the building. Business executives who don't have three or four prearranged exits are something I've seen much too often. This has reduced the worth of the firm and even strained family ties.

A business plan enables you to determine the direction your firm is taking, how it will deal with any challenges that may arise, and what it will take to sustain it. When you're prepared to write anything down, utilize a free template as guidance.

3. Evaluate your financial situation.

It requires money to start a business, therefore you must decide how you will pay for it. Will you need to borrow money or do you have the resources to finance your startup? Do you have enough funds to go by till you turn a profit if you want to quit your job to concentrate on your business? Identify the beginning fees that you will incur.

Since they run out of money before making a profit, many businesses fail. It's never a bad idea to anticipate your beginning costs because it may take some time before the company starts to generate stable income.

Analyze the break-even point.
A break-even analysis is one method you may use to figure out how much money you need. This crucial component of financial planning aids business owners in estimating the profitability of their enterprise, item, or service.

The method is easy:

assemble a team
Fixed Costs ÷ (Average Price Per Unit − Variable Costs) = Break-Even Point
This formula should be used as a tool by every entrepreneur since it indicates the minimal level of

performance required for your company to break even. Also, it enables you to determine exactly where your revenues originate so that you may adjust your production targets.

Following are the top three justifications for performing a break-even analysis:

Calculate profitability. The primary interest of every business owner is often this.
How much income will I need to produce to pay for all of my expenses? Which goods or services are profitable, and which are lost-making?

A product or service's price. The majority of individuals think about the cost of production and price when deciding how much to charge for their goods.
Find out the fixed rates, variable charges, and overall cost by asking yourself these questions. What are the prices of any tangible goods? How much does labor cost?

Review the data. Think about how many products or services you would need to sell to make a profit.
How can I lower my overall fixed costs, you ask? How can I lower the unit variable costs? How can my sales increase?

Monitor your spending.

Don't start a business by overspending. Recognize the kinds of investments that are sensible for your company, and stay away from overpaying on expensive new equipment that won't advance your company's objectives. Make sure you are on track by keeping an eye on your business spending.

"Many companies tend to waste money on pointless things," "We worked with a small firm that only had two workers, but they spent a lot of money on office space that could accommodate twenty. Also, they rented a high-end professional printer that was better equipped for a crew of 100 and came with key cards to monitor who was printing what and when. Spend as little as possible at first, and only on what is necessary for the firm to develop and prosper. When you're established, you can afford the luxury.

Think about your financial possibilities.

Your business's start-up cash may come from several sources. The ideal technique to obtain finance for your company relies on several variables, including creditworthiness, the required sum, and the possibilities accessible.

Commercial loans. A business loan from a bank is a smart place to start if you need money, however, they are sometimes challenging to obtain. Apply for a small business loan through the S. Small Business Administration (SBA) or an alternative lender if you are unable to obtain a bank loan.

grants for companies. Grants for businesses are comparable to loans but do not require repayment. Business grants frequently have strict requirements that must be met for the firm to be considered. Look for small company grants that are tailored to your needs when applying for one. Government funds, grants for women-owned enterprises, and grants for minority-owned firms are available options.

Companies that need a sizable amount of money upfront might wish to enlist the help of an angel investor. Investors are willing to give a startup firm several million dollars or more in exchange for a direct hand in managing your company.

As an alternative, you may start an equity crowdfunding campaign to get support from many people for lesser amounts of money. Several businesses have benefited from crowdfunding in recent years, and there are hundreds of trustworthy platforms available for all kinds of organizations.

Our guide to startup financing possibilities has further information on each of these cash sources.

Choose the ideal business bank.
Size is important when selecting a corporate bank. Because they are aware of the regional market circumstances and will work with you based on your entire business profile and character, I advise considering smaller community banks.

They are not like huge banks, which consider your credit score and will be pickier about who they lend money to.

Also, local banks want to get to know you personally so they can assist you if you experience difficulties and miss a payment. Smaller banks also have the advantage of having decisions made at the branch level, which can be quicker than at a higher level in larger banks.

While selecting a bank for your company, you should ask yourself the following questions:

What matters most to me?
Do I want to establish a close relationship with a bank that is eager to lend me support in any way?

Do I want to be seen by major banks as simply another bank account?
selecting your providers

The best bank for your company ultimately depends on your demands. You may focus your search by outlining your banking requirements in writing. To pick the finest bank for your company, set up appointments with several and inquire about how they assist small companies.

When it comes to money, you should do a break-even analysis, think about your costs and funding choices, and pick the best bank for your company.

4. Choose the legal framework for your company.

Determine the type of entity your firm is in before registering it. Your legal business structure has an impact on a variety of factors, including your tax filing strategy and your potential personal liabilities.

Single proprietorship: If you want to be alone liable for all debts and responsibilities and independently control the firm, you may choose to register as a sole proprietorship. Be advised that using this path may negatively impact your credit.

Alternative: A business partnership, as its name suggests, is one in which two or more persons are jointly and severally accountable as the company's owners. If you can locate a business partner with abilities that complement your own, you don't have to do it alone. Adding someone to the mix typically makes sense if you want your firm to succeed.

Consider the benefits and drawbacks of companies if you wish to separate your obligation from that of your firm (e.g., an S corporation or C corporation). Although each form of company is subject to a particular set of rules, this legal framework often creates a business that is distinct from its owners. As a result, companies have the same legal rights as people to own property, bear responsibility, pay taxes, enter into contracts, and bring legal action. "Corporations, particularly C corporations, are particularly ideal for young enterprises that expect to "go public" or seek venture capital backing soon,"

Limited liability company: The limited liability company is one of the most used organizational forms for small enterprises (LLC). This hybrid organization combines the tax advantages of a partnership with the legal security of a corporation.

The choice of an entity type is ultimately up to you based on your present requirements and long-term business objectives. Understanding the many legal business formats that are available is crucial. If you're having trouble deciding, it's a good idea to talk it over with a business or legal expert.

A legal business structure, such as a sole proprietorship, partnership, corporation, or limited liability company (LLC), must be chosen.

5. Register with the IRS and the government.

Before you may legally operate your firm, you must get the necessary business licenses. You have to register your company, for instance, with the federal, state, and municipal governments. Before enrolling, you need to gather several papers.

incorporating documents and operating agreements You must register with the government to be recognized as a legal business entity. Articles of incorporation, which must include your company's name, mission, corporate structure, stock information, and other characteristics, are required for corporations. Similarly to this, certain LLCs must draft an operating agreement.

Doing business as (DBA)

You must register your business name, which can be your legal name, a fake DBA name (if you are the sole proprietor), or the name you have chosen for your firm if you don't have articles of incorporation or an operating agreement. For further legal protection, you might also wish to take measures to trademark your company name.

Most states mandate that you obtain a DBA. If you're in a general partnership or a single proprietorship that uses a fake name, you might need to file for a DBA certificate. To learn more about the particular criteria and costs, call or contact the county clerk's office in your area. In most cases, there is a registration cost.

Organizational identification number (EIN)

You might need to obtain an employer identification number from the IRS following the registration of your firm. Although it is not necessary for sole proprietorships without workers, you could still wish to apply to keep your personal and company taxes separate or to spare yourself the hassle if you decide to hire someone in the future. To evaluate if you need an EIN to operate your business, the IRS has published a checklist. You may register for a free EIN online if you do.

IRS tax documents
To complete your federal and state income tax requirements, you must file specific forms. The paperwork you require depends on the structure of your organization. To learn more about state-specific and municipal tax duties, visit the website of your state. The greatest online tax software can assist you with filing and paying your taxes quarterly and annually once you've set everything up.

The owner of NPL Consulting and licensed attorney Natalie Pierre-Louis stated, "You could be tempted to wing it with a PayPal account and social networking platform, but if you start with a strong foundation, your business will have fewer obstacles to worry about in the long run."

Federal, State, and Local Permits
Certain firms can additionally need licenses and permissions from the federal, state, or municipal governments to function. The best place to get a business license is at your town hall. The SBA's database may then be used to look for state and business-type license requirements.

In several trades, businesses and independent contractors are obliged to have professional licenses. A professional business license is something like a commercial driver's license (CDL). Buses, tank trucks, and tractor-trailers are just a few of the vehicles that someone with a CDL is allowed to drive. Three classes—Class A, Class B, and Class C—are used to categorize CDLs.

You should also inquire with your city and state to see whether a seller's permit is required so that your company may legally charge and collect sales tax from clients. Resell permission, permit license, reseller permit, resale ID, state tax ID number, reseller number, reseller license permit, or certificate of authority are some of the several names for a seller's permit.

It's crucial to remember that each state has its standards and names. Using the state government website of the state or states you are conducting business in, you may apply for a seller's permit.

Not all companies are required to gather sales tax or acquire a seller's license.

For instance, most services (such as professional services, education, and capital renovations to real estate), medications, and food for domestic use are typically exempt from the New York sales tax requirement. So, you do not require a New York seller's permit if your company simply sells medications. Nevertheless, the sale of brand-new tangible personal property, utilities, telephone service, hotel stays, and food and drink (in restaurants) must be accompanied by the collection of New York sales tax.

Register important papers such as operational agreements, articles of incorporation, DBAs, EINs, income tax returns, and other necessary licenses and permissions.

6. Invest in an insurance plan.

The correct insurance for your business should be purchased before you formally begin, but you may forget about it as something you want to do someday. It can be expensive to deal with situations like property damage, theft, or even a consumer lawsuit, so you need to be sure you're adequately insured.

There are a few fundamental insurance plans that the majority of small firms may take advantage of, even though you should think about a variety of business insurance options. For instance, if your company plans to hire staff, you will at the very least need to get workers' compensation and unemployment insurance.

Depending on your region and sector, you could also require additional forms of coverage, although the majority of small companies are advised to have general liability (GL) insurance, commonly known as a company owner's policy. Property damage, bodily harm, and personal injury to you or a third party are all covered by GL.

If your company offers a service, professional liability insurance can also be something you desire. It protects you if you act improperly or fail to take necessary action while running your firm.

7. Develop your team.

To launch your business, you'll need to assemble a fantastic staff, unless you want to be its sole employee. Entrepreneurs must pay equal attention to the "people" aspect of their company as they do to their products.

People make your product, thus it should be your top responsibility to identify your founding team, recognize any gaps, and plan how and when to fill them. Equally crucial is figuring out how the team will function as a whole. You'll save a lot of problems later on if you define roles and duties, the division of labor, how to provide feedback, and how to collaborate when everyone is not in the same room.

8. Choose your suppliers.

You and your team probably won't be able to handle running a firm entirely on your own because it might be challenging. Third-party companies can help with that. Businesses in any sector, whether they specialize in business phone systems or human resources, are there to work with you and make your operation operate more smoothly. For instance, you may create an IVR system for your business phone system to automatically direct callers to the appropriate people.

Choose cautiously while looking for B2B partners. Finding a trustworthy person is essential since these businesses will have access to your most important and perhaps sensitive company information. Our professional sources advised inquiring about possible suppliers' experience in your field, their track record with current clients, and the level of development they have assisted previous clients in achieving in our guide to picking business partners.

Although not every business will require the same kind of suppliers, practically all businesses will require some standard goods and services. Take into account the following operations, which are essential for any kind of business.

Allowing different consumer payment methods: By allowing different payment methods, you may make a sale in whichever format your target customer finds simplest. To be sure you're receiving the greatest cost for your business, compare alternatives to locate the best credit card processing company. This is because accepting credit cards for small businesses is frequently a quick way to increase sales and clientele.

Setting up a point-of-sale (POS) system will provide you with a cutting-edge user interface for accepting consumer payments. The finest POS systems combine customer and inventory management capabilities with this payment technology, which primarily overlaps with credit card processing. As a result, POS systems are crucial if you intend to sell things rather than provide services.

Handling finances: When a firm first begins, many owners handle their own accounting needs. Nevertheless, as your company expands, you may save time by employing an accountant or by selecting the best accounting software supplier.

9. Promote your brand.

You need to establish your brand and amass a following of clients who are prepared to leap when you open your doors for business, whether they be actual or metaphorical before you start selling your goods or services.

Create a corporate website and capitalize on your internet reputation. A website is digital proof that your small business is real for the many clients who use the internet to research products and services. Also, it is a terrific tool to communicate with both existing and future clients.
Utilize social media to promote your new company. You might use it as a promotional tool to provide followers with deals and discounts after your debut.

Depending on who you are trying to reach, social media sites may not be the ideal option.

CRM: The top CRM solutions provide you the ability to save client information to enhance your marketing to them. When it comes to connecting with your audience and reaching consumers, a well-planned email marketing campaign may be quite effective. Building your email marketing contact list carefully is essential for success.

Have a consistent logo across all of your channels to help customers recognize your business.

Keep your digital assets current with fascinating, pertinent material about your company and sector; far too many entrepreneurs approach their websites incorrectly.

They view their website as an expense rather than an investment, which is the problem. That's a grave error in the modern digital world. Small company entrepreneurs will have an advantage in getting off to a successful start if they recognize how important having a strong internet presence is.

Building a clientele requires developing a marketing strategy that continues after your product launch since it should constantly spread the word about your company. In the beginning, this approach is equally as crucial as offering a high-quality good or service.

Request consumer consent to send them marketing communications.
Ask your current and future clients for their permission to communicate with them as you develop your brand. The use of opt-in permission forms is the simplest approach to do this. With these forms, you may get in touch with them and provide more details about your company.

These kinds of forms are frequently used in e-commerce to ask customers for their consent to send them newsletters, marketing materials, product sales, etc. People receive so many unnecessary emails and other messages these days that by getting them to voluntarily opt into your services, you can start to earn their trust.

Building trust and respect with prospective clients may begin with opt-in forms. More significantly, the use of these forms is mandated by law. The Federal Trade Commission must follow regulations outlined in the CAN-SPAM Act of 2003 for commercial email. This rule applies to all commercial messages, which are defined by the law as "any electronic mail message the principal goal of which is the commercial advertisement or promotion of a commercial product or service." It does not only apply to bulk email. The maximum penalties for any email that violates this rule are $40,000.

Develop a comprehensive marketing campaign that includes many channels of communication, such as a company website, social media, email newsletters, and opt-in forms.

10. Expand your company.

Your duty as an entrepreneur doesn't end with your debut and initial sales. You must constantly expand your company if you want to turn a profit and stay afloat. While doing so requires time and work, you will ultimately get what you put into your business.

An excellent strategy to attain growth is to partner with more well-known businesses in your sector. Make contact with other businesses and request some advertising in return for a free sample of a product or service. Join forces with a charitable organization and donate some of your time or goods to raise awareness of your brand.

There's never a flawless strategy, even though these suggestions can help you establish your firm and make it ready to thrive. When launching a business, you want to make sure you are fully prepared, yet things will most likely go wrong. You must adjust to shifting circumstances if you want to manage a successful firm.

METHODS FOR BEGINNING AND GROWING A PROFITABLE BUSINESS

To thrive in business today, you must be adaptable and possess strong organizing and planning abilities. Many people start businesses with the expectation that they can switch on their computers or open their doors and start producing money, only to discover that doing so is considerably harder than they anticipated.

By taking your time and organizing all the required procedures for success, you may prevent this in your commercial endeavors. You may succeed in your enterprise by applying the following nine suggestions, regardless of the sort of business you intend to launch.

Analytical thinking, resolute organization, and meticulous record-keeping are necessary when starting a firm.

Being aware of your rivals can help you either copy or improve on their winning strategies.

Prepare to make compromises in your personal life when starting your business since you'll almost probably wind up working harder for yourself than you would for someone else.

Gaining your consumers' loyalty and keeping their business requires offering them excellent service.

Make sure that you are as prepared for launch as the business is.

1. Arrange your life

You must be organized if you want to succeed in business. It will assist you in completing activities and maintaining an organized schedule. Making a to-do list every day is a fantastic organizational strategy. Check each thing off your list as you finish it. By doing this, you can be sure that you won't forget anything and will do all the activities required to secure the sustainability of your company.

There are several SaaS technologies available to improve organizations. Slack, Asana, Zoom,

Microsoft Teams, and more recent additions are examples of such tools.

Having said that, a straightforward Excel spreadsheet can do for many organizational needs in a firm.

2. Maintain thorough records

Successful firms all maintain thorough records. You'll be aware of the company's financial situation and any prospective difficulties by doing this. Merely being aware of this offers you the opportunity to develop plans to deal with those difficulties.

The majority of firms opt to maintain two sets of records: one on paper and one online. A firm may stop worrying about data loss by having records that are continuously updated and backed up. The physical record serves as a backup but is most frequently used to confirm the accuracy of the other data.

3. Examine your rivals.

The finest outcomes come from competition. You must not be scared to research and pick up tips from your rivals if you want to succeed. After all, they could be doing something correctly that you can use in your company to increase profits.

The way you evaluate competition will vary by industry. If you run a restaurant, you might be able to get information by simply eating at your rivals' establishments, asking other patrons what they think, and so on. You can, however, be a business with far less access to your rivals, like a chemicals industry. In that case, you would consult a business expert and an accountant to review not only how the company presents itself to the public but also any financial data you may be able to find on it.

4. Recognize the Rewards and Risks

Taking measured risks to advance your company is the key to success. What are the drawbacks is an excellent thing to ask. You will know the worst-case situation if you can respond to this question. You'll be able to take the type of measured risks that may result in enormous profits thanks to this understanding.

Making wise company startup decisions requires an understanding of risks and benefits. For instance, was launching a new restaurant during a period of social isolation and restricted seating an obstacle or an opportunity for you as a result of the severe economic disruption of 2020?

5. Be Creative

Constantly be on the lookout for methods to enhance your company and set it apart from the competition. Acknowledge your limitations and be open to fresh perspectives and alternative business strategies.

Several channels might provide extra income. Amazon is a good example. The business began as a bookshop and developed into a major player in eCommerce. Few people anticipated that Amazon's Web Services section would be a significant source of revenue. When Jeff Bezos decided to stand down as CEO, the head of Amazon Web Services was chosen as the new CEO because the division performed so well.

Remain Concentrated

Rome wasn't built in a day, as the proverb goes. Just starting a business does not guarantee that you will make money right away. Keep your attention on attaining your immediate objectives since it takes time for others to learn who you are.

Many small business owners utilize their profits to pay back investment expenditures for several years before even turning a profit. Being in the red is the term for this. It's referred to as being "in the black" when your business is profitable and you have money left over after paying your bills and employees.

However, if a company is still not making a profit after a considerable amount of time, it may be worthwhile to investigate whether there are problems with the product or service, whether the market is still viable, and any other potential problems that could hinder or even stop a company's expansion.

7. Be Ready to Offer Up Sacrifices
Even though starting a business requires a lot of labor, your work doesn't end when your doors are open. To succeed, you frequently need to put in more time than you would if you were working for someone else, which could include sacrificing quality time with loved ones.

For people who are dedicated to making their firm successful, the proverb "There are no weekends and no vacations for business entrepreneurs" may be accurate. There is nothing wrong with working a full-time job, and several business entrepreneurs overestimate the actual cost of the sacrifices needed to launch and run a successful enterprise.

8. Provide superb service

Many prosperous companies overlook the significance of offering excellent customer service. If you provide your clients superior service, they'll be more likely to choose you over your rivals the next time they need anything.

The quality of the services a company offers frequently makes the difference between successful and failed enterprises in today's very competitive business market. The adage "undersell and overdeliver" is applicable in this situation, and astute business owners would do well to heed it.

9. Be Reliable

Being consistent is essential for company success. You must consistently take the steps required to achieve success. Long-term profitable habits will be formed as a result, helping you earn money.

What Strategy for Company Growth Is Fastest?

Companies will expand at their speeds, and frequently, neither the owner nor the staff has any influence over this. Running a lean operation can, however, have several advantages that can help a firm expand fast. These advantages include concentrating on a narrow product line, scaling up rather than down, and having a clear competitive advantage.

How Do You Boost Sales?
There are several potential sources for rising sales. You may up your advertising budget where it has been shown to work, solicit referrals from current customers, create a direct-to-consumer email list, and other strategies. A product line can also be expanded, but if it performs poorly, it will hurt your bottom line.

What Defines a Successful Startup?
Startups may be a great method to produce returns for stakeholders if business success is defined as providing profits for stakeholders. The top startups offer excellent, scalable products or services. The company is prepared to seize opportunities when they arise, can swiftly pivot, and is aware of the market and its financial status.

conclusion
The U.S. Bureau of Labor Statistics estimates that around 20% of new enterprises fail in their first two years of operation, 45% fail in their first five years, and 65% fail in their first decade. Just 25% of newly founded companies survive for 15 years or more.

These nine suggestions are a fantastic place to start if you want to be one of the 25%, but they are by no means all-inclusive. The nature of running a business requires ongoing learning and adjustment.

UNDERSTANDING BUSINESS FINANCES

Understanding Business Finance Fundamentals
What is finance for businesses? What does it include, exactly? In the end, business financing refers to the process of supporting a business' activities using money from outside the firm. This can be done by borrowing money from a lender, issuing stocks or bonds to investors, or acquiring venture capital.

knowledge of business finance
The world of current finance is not what it used to be, where the finance department exclusively performs accountant-based activities. This is important to keep in mind while trying to comprehend company finance. Instead, it has dramatically changed to encompass a more comprehensive value addition to firms. Because to technological improvements in financial automation, a Chief Financial Officer (CFO) nowadays, for instance, not just focuses on statistics but also provides significant strategy and leadership

to a corporation. Business finance professionals also look after a company's finances as well as the instruments and financial analysis utilized to allocate these financial resources. Corporate finance teams spot any possible financial issues the company could have and then take steps to avoid them. The ultimate objective of finance in business is to increase a company's value through efficient financial planning, resource management, and financial development, while constantly keeping risk and profitability in mind. 5l

With this in mind, the success of a firm depends on how effectively financial tools like loans and investments are used.

One of a corporate finance team's most crucial tasks is to increase the company's financial standing through capital investments.

What actions regulate commerce and finance?
1. Budgeting and investments
A corporation uses capital budgeting, also known as investment assessment, to assess whether a project, such as opening a new branch or purchasing new equipment, would boost the company's value or be profitable. When a project's return on investment

exceeds its capital expenditure, it is said to be profitable.

Corporate finance must have a thorough awareness of the company's present business finances, where the cash is coming from, and how much the firm requires during the planning or budgeting process.

2. Investment funding

One of the most crucial business operations of a finance team is expanding the company's financial position through capital investments. There are two kinds of capital for businesses that require financing:

Fixed capital is used to acquire the business's permanent assets, such as real estate, buildings, and machinery.

Typically, working capital is used to purchase raw materials and control fixed costs like overhead and salaries.

Financial resources including shares, debentures, banks, financial institutions, the sale of stock for equity financing, and creditors are frequently used to raise company funding. To ensure that there is enough liquidity for the company to conduct day-to-day operations, corporate finance also monitors the short-term financial management of the company.

3. Capital gains and dividends

For a corporation to maximize value growth, the way it arranges its capital is crucial. Based on the ratio between a company's liabilities and equity funding, one may establish if it is a risk or a well-balanced enterprise.

The days of corporate finance staff maintaining records and balancing the books are numbered as artificial intelligence and machine learning gain traction in commercial finance.

4. Debt Financing

In the process of business debt financing, a company borrows money from a lender and gives the lender a share of the company in exchange. The firm is then responsible for repaying the loan's principal as well as any accumulated interest. Many factors may lead a company to use business debt financing:

To grow their firm by purchasing additional machinery, real estate, or adding more staff To pay for ongoing expenditures when they don't have enough cash on hand to restructure a current loan and obtain a better interest rate

Many business finance careers

As a company finance specialist, you will normally offer impartial financial advice to a variety of customers, including governments, private businesses, and people in addition to corporations and financial investors.

1. Private equity

When a business sells shares of ownership (i.e., equity) to investors to obtain money for its operations, this is known as equity financing or funding. Private equity firms assist enterprises that want more funding in raising it. A private equity corporation provides funding to the business directly in exchange for an ownership stake, unlike banks that accomplish this via selling shares or corporate bonds.

"A successful private equity profession needs both interpersonal and quantitative abilities. The capacity to handle numbers quickly and effectively is known as mathematical aptitude. Nevertheless, interpersonal relationships are also crucial. Companies are ultimately about people and their personalities, therefore understanding the human aspect is also necessary for success in the private equity industry.

2. Business development

Corporate development careers involve coordinating and carrying out mergers, negotiating acquisitions, carrying out divestitures, and making sure that business capital is obtained internally.

3. Treasury

Treasury is in charge of the company's capital and controls its liquidity and risk through cash flow forecasting, working capital management, and upkeep of credit lines.

Additional responsibilities include managing consumer credit, investing money and pension funds, and putting procedures in place to govern treasury activities while reporting back to management on the company's liquidity and financial situation.

4. Investment banking

Most entry-level investment bankers begin as financial analysts and careers in investment banking often start with an internship. Investment bankers assist firms in creating plans to seek extra funding. This can be done by issuing and selling securities, by disclosing crucial data on the financial standing and health of businesses via mergers, acquisitions, and other financial transactions, or by any other means.

If you're interested in a career in finance, you have a wide range of possibilities to choose from, including the business finance job pathways mentioned above. Making wise decisions for your company's finances requires staying informed about the most recent trends and developments in the business world, which is always changing and developing. Understanding the fundamentals of finance will help you establish yourself as a professional with the abilities required to work with both large and small, public and private firms.

The days of corporate finance staff maintaining records and balancing the books are numbered as artificial intelligence and machine learning gain traction in commercial finance.

20 Whether it's for operating a small firm or a major corporation, corporate finance is now more important than ever for assisting decision-makers in making knowledgeable business decisions. With their access to new software integrations, corporate finance can evaluate data trends, pose the

appropriate inquiries, and provide crucial information about the company's financials, allowing them to address actual business issues.

CONTROLLING AND EXPANDING YOUR CLIENT BASE

Owners of businesses are constantly seeking new methods to expand their clientele. The possibility of selling to an existing client is 60–70% compared to the chance of selling to a new prospect, which is 5-20%, thus they also concentrate on keeping existing customers.

But despite current technology, company owners still struggle to come up with efficient strategies to attract and keep clients.

In this article, we'll explain what a client base is and offer advice on how your business may expand and keep its current one.

What is a customer base?
The population of people who often utilize the goods and services provided by your business is known as your customer base. These clients interact with your firm regularly and bring in the greatest money. Your client base may consist of a particular

group or a target population based on a buyer profile, depending on the industry.

Knowing who your consumer base is is crucial since they are a huge asset to your company. These are the ones that rely on your business to help them reach their objectives and buy your items the most. Your marketing, sales, and customer support teams can better connect with your customer base by identifying these customers.

Your installed customer base is a smaller group of clients inside your customer base. These consumers stand out from the rest of your customer base because they are in a particular stage of the customer journey.

Installed Base vs. Consumer Base
The segment of your client base that is actively utilizing your products is referred to as the installed base. Contrary to the client base, this group does not include those who have not made a purchase in the past or are not taking advantage of the offers given by your company. By identifying these clients, your business can offer prompt service and increase customer retention.

For instance, everyone who has purchased or utilized one of HubSpot's free or paid offerings would be considered a customer.

Yet, the only users of HubSpot's products in daily workflow would make up the company's installed base. We may tailor our marketing, sales, and customer service offers to meet the unique demands of our active users by emphasizing this segment of our client base.

While acquiring leads is crucial for growing a client base, it is insufficient to expand your installed base. Choose the best strategy for balancing lead generation and client retention if you want your firm to succeed, and both your installed base and customer base will increase.

You could be asking how to create, expand, and keep one now that you can identify your installed base and client base. Let's investigate.

Ways to Increase Your Customer Base
Here are a few straightforward methods you may use to begin expanding your clientele from scratch.

1. Increase brand recognition on social media.

You may start growing your consumer base and disseminating information about your company on social media for little to no money.

With websites like Facebook, LinkedIn, and Instagram, you can rapidly engage with your audience. You can even hold contests to draw in additional visitors.

2. Collaborate with other companies.
Partnering with other companies is a certain strategy to increase your consumer base if your firm is still relatively young and has a small customer base.

You must provide something worthwhile in exchange for the larger client base you're attempting to reach for the relationship to succeed.

To assist their clients in documenting their outdoor excursions, hikes, or workouts, for instance, you may execute a co-marketing campaign with an outdoor or fitness company if you offer portable cameras.

3. Implement email marketing initiatives.
Email is still one of the best ways for companies to begin expanding their consumer base. The

individuals on your email list are already interested in your goods and services, unlike those on social media.

To nurture these leads until they become clients, establish email marketing campaigns.
So let's think about ways to expand your consumer base.

Ways to Expand Your Client base
Customer service teams expand and keep your client base by delivering a wonderful customer experience, while marketing and sales teams are crucial in bringing in and engaging your consumers.

This endeavor encourages repeat business from clients and opens up prospects for upselling and cross-selling. The customer care staff can employ the strategies listed below to increase and keep your client base.

1. Provide first-rate customer service.
Although it may seem straightforward, many businesses fall short of providing great customer service. In fact, according to studies, 80% of customers have discontinued doing business with a brand as a result of bad customer service.

Consumers want perfection, and even a single slip-up by your business might cause a turnover.

Your staff should see dealing with needy or dissatisfied clients as a chance to expand your customer base rather than as a burden. Responding quickly to client concerns will enhance the likelihood that they will buy your items again.

Customer retention is significantly influenced by customer service as well. According to studies, 91% of customers who receive good customer service will make another purchase. Naturally, this increases the pressure on your customer support personnel to quickly satisfy the client's request.

2. Promote client loyalty.
It might be difficult to draw in new clients for your company, particularly if they are unfamiliar with your goods or services.

Customers are also wary of commercials, and the majority won't be convinced by your marketing efforts alone. Instead, customers must have faith that your business shares and cares about their objectives.

Using your customer advocates is one of the finest strategies to earn the confidence of new prospects. These brand evangelists offer recommendations and endorsements that raise the reputation of your company.

According to a BrightLocal study, 79% of shoppers believe internet evaluations are just as reliable as personal recommendations. As a result, even if your customer advocates aren't immediately generating new leads, encouraging and sharing their opinions will raise the credibility of your business.

3. Create freemium deals.
Freemium deals are an excellent method to draw in new customers. A freemium offer is when a business offers something valuable in return for consumer data. The freebie might be as straightforward as a PDF download or more engaging, like a demo version of a program.

For instance, HubSpot provides a freemium version of its customer support, sales, and marketing capabilities. Although there is no cost associated with using these tools, users must provide an email address and register for a HubSpot account.

Customers may experience how helpful HubSpot tools can be for their company in this way. To provide targeted customer care and sales offers based on the tools these people use most frequently, HubSpot may evaluate the product use data for these users.

4. Use customer service resources.
Your customer care staff needs to change as you gain more clients to accommodate the rise in client demand. Hire extra representatives to handle support inquiries as one of your company's options.

This method is less ideal, though, because it requires a lot of money and time to finish. Instead of recruiting more staff, you may increase the capacity of your customer care team by using customer service solutions.

A help desk is one resource you may add to your customer care team. A knowledge base, a ticketing system, and a shared inbox are just a few of the useful customer care features that may be found on a help desk platform. Incoming service requests are automatically distributed and organized by these technologies, making it simpler for representatives to handle their open cases. Customer service tools streamline your reps' workflow and provide them with more time so they may take on more cases each day without having to keep track of what they are working on.

5. Get client opinions.
Look at your customer reviews if you're at a loss on how to draw in more clients.

Good feedback reveals your strengths and what you should brag about to potential customers. Negative feedback reveals areas for improvement and changes that must be made to boost client retention.

You may get a better understanding of what your target market appreciates most about your business by closely monitoring the feedback you receive from customers.

After a customer service encounter or the conclusion of a support issue, service feedback should be gathered. Once a client makes a purchase, you may also ask them for feedback since you could be interested in how well your sales team on the sales floor is handling customer service issues.

There are numerous efficient methods for gathering customer feedback. Give customers surveys, for instance, following a transaction or service interaction.

Since they give your business both qualitative and quantitative information about your clients, surveys are excellent. Check out some of these methods to get customer feedback if your team is having trouble getting responses.

6. Create a program for customer success.
Successful companies are aware that a customer's worth rises with each subsequent purchase they make from you. Thus even if you just bring in a small number of consumers each month, if you can persuade them to return to your establishment, your customer base will increase steadily.

A customer success program is one technique that can help with client retention. Teams responsible for customer success keep an eye out for obstacles in each client's path. If they foresee friction, they may get in touch with the consumer and assist them in resolving the matter before it becomes a major issue.

When you can eliminate pain points before customers ever become aware of them, this may make a huge impact in reducing customer turnover.

7. Keep web accessibility in mind.
If you have a website, it's important to remember that not everyone uses the internet in the same manner, making your brand accessible to anybody with internet access.

For certain individuals to utilize and access your website successfully, their computers must have particular features enabled. This audience cannot see your material if your site is incompatible with these programs, which means you are losing out on possibilities to convert potential leads.

Online accessibility may provide your company access to a hitherto untapped eCommerce market.

8. Make your client loyalty program even better.
Your customer loyalty program is yet another effective tool for attracting and retaining customers. When clients contrast your business with a rival in your industry, it may provide you with a competitive edge. It can also keep your most devoted customers interested in your brand's promotional offerings.

When choosing a new brand, 69% of customers think loyalty programs have an impact on their choice.

Using a tiered membership structure is one method to improve your customer loyalty program. When consumers advance through each level of loyalty, tiers encourage them to keep doing business with you and foster a feeling of community.

When clients go to the top tier, the incentives should get more valuable and should have unique tiers. Here, your team may calculate client lifetime value and figure out how much a customer must spend with you before they qualify as one of your most devoted patrons.

9. Make the shopping experience more fun.
Gamification is the technique of incorporating entertaining features into routine chores or procedures to make the process more fun or interesting.

Companies are now using gamified features that improve their client experience to attract new consumers. Customers are expected to love using the product and desire to keep using it since it reminds them of a pastime or game.

10. Make customer onboarding personalized.
The few seconds that follow a client purchasing with your brand are crucial to their journey.

They could completely forgo utilizing your product and go for a more user-friendly substitute if they have trouble using it or comprehending the user manual. Since they were unable to use a product, 55% of customers have returned it.

This issue may be resolved by your client onboarding program by tailoring each user's experience. Have your staff seek out your consumers to learn more about their unique wants and goals rather than using a one-size-fits-all strategy.

Customers will know exactly how to contact you if they have questions if you prominently advertise your customer service choices on the packaging of any retail products you sell. To deliver dependable, in-the-moment help, you must make your customer care personnel available to them.

Customer Base Illustrations

After learning how to create and expand a client base, let's look at some typical customer base instances.

1. Consistent Clients

They are clients that have been making purchases from your company over time. They now adore your goods and services and would be happy to recommend your company to others.

Without a doubt, it's important to focus extra attention on this clientele. By maintaining or raising the caliber of your goods and services, you can keep them happy. Start a loyalty program to thank these clients for their steadfast business.

2. New Clients

Those who recently purchased from your shop are considered new consumers.

Making sure new customers have all they need to succeed with the product or service they just purchased is a terrific way to convert them into recurrent or loyal consumers.

If your company sells things, give prospective clients manuals or instructions that go into great depth about how to use the products. Moreover, if your company provides services, you must design unique onboarding processes for different clients.

3. Prospective clients

Although they are not yet clients, it is nevertheless important to pay attention to them. This group is probably still looking into whether your goods and services may help them with their problems.

By developing freemium offerings that provide potential clients with a sample of your goods and services, you can tailor them to them.

4. Bargain/Discount Customers

These clients are neither brand-new nor devoted. Instead, they only show up when you're running a promotion or a deal.

It is wise to avoid concentrating too much on this clientele because they are quick to switch brands when one provides a greater discount.

It's time to expand your clientele

It's challenging to increase and keep your consumer base. Yet, you too can create a clientele that will ensure steady sales for your company if you use the appropriate channels and techniques.

CHAPTER 5:

MARKETING AND BRANDING

Discovering the Distinction Between Branding and Marketing

Have you ever thought about how branding and marketing differ from one another? If so, you're not the only one. Even while there is no question that the two are related, there are little variances between the two.

To combine branding and marketing successfully, you must have a thorough understanding of both as a business owner. An examination of the distinctions between branding and marketing is provided below.

Branding: What Is It?

In a nutshell, branding refers to who you are, while marketing refers to the process of raising awareness. Marketing includes your tactical objectives, whereas branding is your strategy. You need to ask yourself several questions to identify your brand. Inquiries that go beyond generalizations about the sector, the services or goods provided, and include inquiries into your identity as a business and, more crucially, your identity as a brand. The following inquiries are a great place to start:

What are your fundamental beliefs and values?
What is the gist of your mission?
What motivated you to launch your company?
Why do you want to make your goods or services available to your intended market?
What distinguishes you?
What is the corporate culture at your company?
What kind of style would you use in the workplace?
What traits do you have in terms of communication?
When someone hears the name of your company, what do you want them to think of?
What emotions do you want customers to have when they think about your company?
How do you want your business to be seen by its clients?

You can better grasp the differences between branding and marketing by responding to the questions above. Spend time crafting detailed responses, then test them out on your peers and professional mentors. You'll note that every question is about the internal processes and culture of your company. As a result, what you create within will eventually manifest outside.

What your customers may anticipate from you and what they will feel while using your products or services will be cultivated by your branding. Your branding may thus be used to precede and support your marketing initiatives by clearly describing who you are, both now and in the future.

What Is Marketing?
When comparing marketing with branding, marketing refers to the methods you use to spread your brand's message. The items and services you offer will also continue to alter and evolve, just like marketing will do. Marketing will promote your brand's basic principles while being directly and specifically targeted to segments of your target demographic.

The field of marketing is enormous. It might be hilarious, serious, or sincere. Any combination of text, keywords, images, pictures, graphs, and videos can be used. Many online and offline techniques will be used for marketing, with some of the more popular ones being:

SEO
Social Media Marketing
Pay Per Click Marketing
Mobile Marketing
Television
Radio
Print campaigns

Yet, there are a lot of additional online and offline marketing strategies you should think about including in your advertising plan. Your brand will never change, even though marketing strategies come and go and the ones you use may alter significantly from year to year or season to season.

Which is more important, branding or marketing?
Your marketing strategy's foundation is your brand, thus branding must come first. When you start coming up with your unique marketing approaches, tools, plans, and tactics, it is crucial to establish your brand's identity precisely, even if you are a startup.
Your brand is the cornerstone on which you will establish customer loyalty and what will keep your customers coming back for more. The brand is what draws repeat business from clients, whether they are independent owned-businesses or large corporations in your neighborhood. Think about

where you order and pick up your family's and your prescription medications as an example. You have probably been a customer of the pharmacy or drugstore where you shop for many years, regardless of whether it is independently owned or a part of a bigger chain. Although you could get the same medicines at any other drugstore in town, it is their brand recognition that draws you in repeatedly.

While marketing strategies may change as they adapt to market conditions and social and cultural changes, branding will never change. Even if you do alter your brand, it is usually in reaction to business expansion or the addition of new services; it is uncommon to completely change your underlying beliefs, objectives, or core values.

Your branding may contain qualities like a strong dedication to quality, community, convenience, communication, or a persistent commitment to meeting a particular need that your target audience has.

Also, bear in mind that branding is something you and your staff must do every day, along with processing every transaction, fielding every contact, and responding to every email. Your marketing, however, is most frequently wholly or partially outsourced to marketing experts. When comparing branding and marketing, branding refers to who you are, whilst marketing refers to how you draw in customers. Consider branding as a strategy to retain current clients and marketing as a way to bring in new ones.

The One Region Marketing And Branding Crossover

There is one instance where branding and marketing are similar even if they are fundamentally different. Branding and marketing are combined when choosing visuals that will be used frequently. A picture, as they say, is worth a thousand words. In light of this, keep in mind that your company's colors, graphics, and logo must first reflect your brand but will also be an important part of your continuous marketing strategy.

The Value Of Branding And Marketing Understanding

If you can now clearly distinguish between marketing and branding but are still not sure why it is important to comprehend the two, the answer is conversions. Your conversions will be lower if your customers do not feel a connection to your brand, even if you base your marketing strategy only on keyword trends and the most successful marketing techniques used in your sector.

What creates an eternal link is your branding. Continuing branding is what keeps people coming back, even if your present marketing strategies are intended to engage. Some businesses provide similar products and services, or even the same ones as yours, thus there is severe competition in this market. Your company's brand will keep customers coming back for more. Your branding is what creates brand loyalty and trust. Your brand is what makes you distinctive.

You could succeed without branding, but your success will be far more significant if you do. Understanding the distinction between marketing and branding will enable you to construct your base of branding—and your expansions via marketing. All great buildings have a solid beginning point and foundation.

CREATING A STRONG BRAND

You must develop strategies to differentiate yourself from the competition with a strong brand-building approach. Find out how to build a brand.

Without a doubt, a well-known and cherished brand is among a company's most important assets. 59% of consumers said they prefer to purchase new goods from well-known companies.

You can be up against large corporations with loyal followings and limitless marketing resources as a small business. You must thus discover methods to stand out by developing a strong brand-building strategy of your own.

Building a brand, not simply a business, is my favorite piece of advice for every entrepreneur.
This is what will lead to your rapid growth and devoted followers.

How does one create a brand?
There is much more to branding than just a catchy logo or strategically placed advertisement.
More has to be done.

What is a brand?
Simply, a customer's entire opinion of your company determines your brand.
"What other people say about you while you're not in the room is your brand,"
Your reputation is your brand!

A strong brand in today's market must be consistent across various applications in its communication and experience:

Environment (storefront or office) (storefront or office)
Print collateral, signage, packaging
Internet marketing and websites
content creation
Customer service and sales
site Internal (with workers) (with employees)
Now, is brand building straightforward? In actuality, branding doesn't take place in an instant or even a few months.

Developing a brand is undoubtedly a process that needs planning. Yet perseverance will pay off in the form of enduring connections with your clients.
As a result, you may see a continuous rise in leads and purchases as well as recommendations from friends and family and advocacy for your goods and services.
The general impression a consumer has of your company shapes your brand.

What is brand development?
Building a brand is defined as increasing public awareness of your company through strategies and

campaigns to establish a distinctive and long-lasting reputation in the market.

Positive image + standing out = brand success.

Three broad stages may be identified in the branding process:

Branding Technique
Brand Identity
brand promotion

Your brand strategy will illustrate how your ideal consumer will see you as unique, reliable, memorable, and likable. It will communicate your goals, commitments, and approach to helping others.

This is THE first step you must do when building a brand from scratch (whether you are just starting or already established).
Without a design or plans, you wouldn't construct a house, right?
The same holds for your brand.

Consider brand strategy to be the road map for how you want the public to perceive your company.

As part of the process, an efficient and thorough brand strategy should incorporate the following elements:

Brand purpose development
audiences' growth
competitor analysis
Brand personality & voice
Brand narrative and messaging
An essential and fundamental component of creating a great brand is brand strategy. Since they go directly into design and marketing, most organizations neglect this area.

The way you communicate this to the audience through imagery, message, and experiences is through brand identity. For maximum impact, match your identity with your mission following your brand strategy.

Consistently implementing your brand identity components across all mediums is important. It's how people start to recognize your company.

You are included in this:
Fonts and colors for logos
Icons and patterns
Website design for collateral Content and message

Advertising
packaging or printing

Brand marketing is a technique used by companies and organizations to draw attention to and raise awareness of their goods and services by linking their values and brand to the appropriate audience through tactful communication.

Using a variety of digital marketing initiatives, you may successfully amplify your brand's image:
user encounter (i.e. your website)
Content marketing and SEO
Use of social media
Email Promotion
Paid Promotion (PPC)

These channels work together to make a company more well-known and help it flourish. Later, we'll go further into each of these components.
To assist your company brand or personal brand develop a more devoted audience, I've streamlined the approach for a thorough brand creation method below.

Do you have any idea where to begin?

How to Create a Loved Brand

1. Discover the purpose behind your brand.
Every successful company has a compelling reason for existing.
And you also ought to.

With your product or service, it's what you wake up enjoying doing for other people (and the globe).
While developing a brand mission, you should consider the following four questions:

Why do you exist?
What makes you unique?
What issue do you address?
Why should people care?
These concepts will serve as the basis for your branding strategy, which will include a tagline, slogans, value propositions, voice, messaging, storytelling, and more.

According to studies, 50% of customers globally claim they increasingly base their purchases on a company's brand effect and values.
So delve deep and uncover the truths that will set your brand apart from the competition.

The Golden Circle model, created by leadership guru Simon Sinek, is a powerful tool for understanding the motivation behind anything in life or business.

The Golden Circle Has 3 Parts:
What – the products or services you offer to your customers
How - the elements that set you apart from the competition
Why: The motivation behind your passion and the reason you exist.
Sinek discusses how to authentically identify a business in the video you'll watch below.

Even after seeing this presentation more than a hundred times, I still get goosebumps. Before our meeting to begin the brand discovery process, I email it to every client.
I disagree with others in the marketing sector who believe this idea is overrated. It's motivating, especially if you're new to branding a company or concept.

It is one of the most-watched TED presentations of all time for a reason, too.
Sit back and observe:

"People purchase why you do things, not what you do, not what you do.

Not every customer needs what you have needed to be a business partner.

Dealing with people who share your beliefs is the objective.

You may utilize The Golden Circle as a jumping-off point to figure out what makes your brand special.

2. Examine the brands of your industry's rivals.

Never copy exactly what the leading companies in your sector are doing.

Yet you should be conscious of what they excel in (or where they fail).

To stand out from the competition is the aim. Persuade a buyer to buy from you rather than your rival!

We always consider methods to differentiate a brand from the competition. Do not omit this stage of brand development.

Do some research on your top rivals or reference brands. For instance, look at how skillfully they established their brand.

A brand name must be simple for customers to identify and remember to be successful.

making a spreadsheet for brand competitor research

A crucial part of developing your brand is conducting competitor research. Make a spreadsheet of brand competitors to compare them first. Excel, Google Sheets, or even just a notepad are all options.

Then, respond to these key inquiries.

Is the rival's visual identity and messaging consistent across channels?

What is the caliber of the goods or services offered by the rivals?
Are there any client testimonials or social media remarks regarding the rival that you can read?
What strategies does the rival use to promote their company both online and off?
Select two to four (2-4) rivals to include in your comparison table. Consider comparing your company to national brands or even looking at similar local enterprises.

One of the main elements in identifying and establishing your brand positioning is competitor research (or market research).

3. Identify the target market for your brand.

Identifying your target demographic will provide the groundwork for developing your brand.

Do you realize that you cannot satisfy everyone's needs?

Keep in mind your target audience when developing your brand. Your purpose and message will be customized to match their specific needs.

The secret is to be precise. Determine the specific habits and way of life of your customers.

I'll give a few succinct examples to illustrate.

There is space to be more descriptive if you are marketing to "college kids." "College students studying abroad in Europe throughout the summer," for instance.

There is little doubt that "Everyone who wants a job" is not a niche audience. Yet it can be for "retirees wishing to return to the workforce in an executive role"

As you can see, focusing on a specialization initially entails making a highly focused commitment.

You'll come to understand that focusing on a smaller segment of your target market gives your company a competitive advantage when branding.

By doing this, you can make sure that the intended audience receives your marketing message in its entirety.

Get a clear image of your target audience before learning how to develop a brand identity that they can relate to.

Your Brand Buyer Persona

A true understanding of the customer persona is essential for brand design. Here are a few details to include in your description of your ideal client:

age, gender, location, income, and level of education.

Go into these specifics to further define the consumer persona for your brand:

Motivations
Goals
Pain points
Fears
Desires
Influencers
Affinities to brands

The process of developing your brand will be affected and benefited by determining who the target market is for your goods or services, especially your marketing initiatives.

You want the perfect customer to read your articles, click on your advertising, join your email list, etc.

Determining your company's target customer base can therefore enhance your entire digital brand-building initiatives. It's unquestionably a crucial initial move!

Keep in mind your target audience when developing your brand. Adapt your goals and messaging to their unique requirements.

4. Define the goal and vision of your brand.
Have you given your brand's purpose and vision any thought? In essence, you'll need to create a crystal-clear statement of the core values of your business.
Your "why" is the reason you wake up each morning.

It's important to understand the value your company offers before you can create a brand that your target market would trust.
Your brand's vision is an aspirational statement for the future that it strives to realize.

Think ten years in the future when you see your brand's future, what it wants to be, and the influence it will have on the environment.

The mission statement serves as a guide for achieving your goal in the here and now, daily. It will guide your brand-building strategy' implementation.
Your purpose and vision should be reflected in every aspect of your brand, including your logo, slogan, voice, message, and personality.

The data gained from The Golden Circle exercise may be used to develop a compelling brand vision and mission statement.

Nike is a good example of a brand.
Nike's catchphrase is well known: Just Do It. Nevertheless, do you know what their mission is?

Nike's mission is: "To bring inspiration and innovation to every athlete in the world".

The Nike mission is evident everywhere. They emphasize how athletes of all stripes use Nike gear to achieve their full potential.

Nike takes their marketing objective a step further by adding the following footnote: "If you have a body, you are an athlete." Imagine how broad their target market would be with such a disclaimer!

The corporation can extend the aim to include every "body" since it has developed such a strong reputation and brand following.

Start small and remember to put your target niche audience first when branding your company.

Your brand loyalty may increase to the point where you may increase your audience.

Let's take a moment to stand back. Check-in with yourself to see whether you've committed to Step 3 of identifying your precise target audience before creating your vision or brand mission statement. It's one of the most crucial elements in the brand-building process overall.
When branding your company, remember to start small and put your target niche audience first.

5. Describe the main attributes and advantages that your brand offers.

There will always be companies that can dominate their field with larger expenditures and greater resources.

Your rights to the goods, services, and benefits are yours alone.

Finding out what you have to offer that no one else does requires serious thought when building a brand that people will remember.

Pay attention to the features and advantages that set your company's branding apart.

Provide your target market with a reason to select your brand over competing ones, supposing you are aware of who they are.

It's critical to remember that this is not only a laundry list of the characteristics your clients or customers can choose from when purchasing your goods or services. Consider how you can add value and make consumers' lives better (outcomes or results that are experienced).

Here are a few illustrations:

improved transparency and authenticity in client service

An improved strategy to boost productivity

lowering expenses by choosing a less expensive alternative

time-saving for routine activities

Apple is a good example of a brand.
Apple is not your average computer manufacturer. Its simplicity of use and simple design are two of its best attributes.

Apple consistently emphasizes to customers that its goods may be utilized immediately out of the box with special packaging and launch events.

Do you recall Apple's catchphrase from 1997 to 2002? Think Different was the slogan. This idea is still prevalent today. List the main attributes and advantages that your brand offers.
Nearly all of the processes involved in developing a brand have been completed. Give yourself a high five if you've made it this far.

6. Create your distinctive brand voice.
The objective, target market, and sector of your business all influence your voice.
It concerns both how you interact with your clients and how they do.

A possible brand voice is:
Professional
Friendly

Service-oriented
Authoritative
Technical
Promotional
Conversational
Informative

Some countless words and variations may develop a brand voice for your marketing.

In the end, you want to pick a brand voice that makes sense to your target audience and resonates with them.

You'll observe that your chances of engaging with customers are greatest if you identify and employ the ideal brand voice.

When posting on social media or a blog, this is very crucial. Your brand's voice will be more easily recognizable across platforms if you keep it consistent. By consuming your material, a community of followers, readers, or subscribers will start to anticipate a certain brand voice and brand personality.

Virgin America is one example of a brand.

Virgin America has a reputation for providing dependable and kind customer service, and it works hard to maintain that reputation.

See their approachable tone on Twitter, where they in this case used comedy depending on location. By guaranteeing power outlets on every flight, they also highlight the value they provide to their clients.

Fish sticks will fly at Pike Place before we ever offer a flight without power outlets. Virgin America (@VirginAmerica), August 4, 2015, "#FleetWide"

Pick a brand voice that makes sense to your target audience and resonates with them.

7. Allow the personality of your brand to shine.
Consumers are not seeking another generic business that does what everyone else does.
They seek a personalized experience that is supported by real human connection.

Do you want to brand your company distinctively? In every step of the brand-building process, make your individuality show.
Use this brand's personality consistently at all points of contact.

Simple examples include: Using "I" and "you" in conversational communication
distributing behind-the-scenes material

telling tales based on actual events
Uniquely describing your goods or services
Make sure your personality stands out in every area
of developing your brand image.

8. Create a brand narrative and messaging.
Explain yourself briefly to buyers while creating a
brand.
Use the corporate tone you've selected for your
brand.

Your messaging should be regularly delivered and
tightly connected to your brand.
Beyond your logo and tagline, this step in
developing your brand defines the essential
elements of:

Your identity
What you provide
What makes people care
A brand narrative gives you the chance to connect
with your audience emotionally and interact on a
human level.

This implies that your language should be easily
comprehended while yet evoking strong feelings.
Be straightforward.

The most essential thing is to focus on why your product is significant to your consumer rather than what it can accomplish when developing a brand story.

Example of a successful brand: TOMS Shoes has amassed a sizable social media following and a resoundingly favorable brand reputation.

On their website, they prominently state their message, "Improving lives. With every product you purchase, TOMS will help a person in need. One for One."
Every interaction a customer has with the brand carries out this narrative.

A brand message gives you the chance to interact with your audience emotionally and on a personal level.

9. Come up with a tagline and brand logo.
Maybe the first thing that comes to mind when you consider brand building is a picture. This far along in the process of developing a brand, we haven't even discussed these!
You might require assistance with the imaginative implementation of this phase.

The process of creating a brand logo and slogan for your business is the most thrilling (and possibly the most crucial component).

This logo will be used in any correspondence with your company. It will serve as your calling card, identification, and visible representation of your commitment.

Therefore be prepared to make the time and financial investment by producing something outstanding to support your company's visual brand.

You want to brand your company. To help your company stand out, work with a professional designer or branding firm that has expertise in creating logos and brand identities.

Their knowledge will guarantee that you receive a distinctive and enduring brand for your company.

To maintain uniformity for any future use of the logo and related brand's color scheme or fonts, a designer may also create brand guidelines.

In a strong brand style guide, the following will be present:

Size and positioning of the logo
Color scheme
Typography and fonts

Iconography
style of photography/image
Web components

Collaborate with a qualified designer or creative agency with experience in branding and identity design to aid in the development of your brand.

10. Include your brand in all facets of your company.
The process of developing a brand never ends.
Everything your consumer can see, read, and hear should reflect your brand and be apparent to them.

I'll explain.
Your brand image should be there when a client enters your office or a customer walks into your store—both in the physical environment and during human encounters.
Your logo must be imprinted on all physical materials, such as business cards, ads, product packaging, and more.

Be sure that your brand appears the same everywhere on digital platforms. To establish consistency with visuals, such as the usage of color and logos, typefaces, photographs, etc., utilize your brand style guide.

The most crucial instrument for promoting your brand is your website. Use your voice, message, and personality in the material while designing your website.

Social media profile pages should reflect your brand aesthetically and in your preferred voice to increase interaction.

And, don't overlook the video! All of these platforms—including YouTube, Facebook Video and Facebook Live, Snapchat, and Instagram Stories—require content that is performed following your brand voice and personality.
Follow a theme that complements your brand's message, value, and voice when you start a podcast.

Warby Parker is a good example of a brand.
In a short period, Warby Parker was able to create a distinctive and superior brand. Its cutting-edge product home try-on experience, retail setting, and digital content marketing initiatives are well suited to its target audience's lifestyle.

Everything your consumer sees (and doesn't see) should reflect your brand and be apparent.

11. Stick to your brand-building principles.

Consistency is essential unless you choose to transform your brand into something more successful based on measurable consumer response.

Every time you need to decide on identification or marketing, refer back to your brand strategy.
Use your brand voice consistently in all of your content after you've established one.
Keep a record of every brand guideline you develop and disseminate for internal use.

If a brand building is inconsistent, what is the point? Don't alter your branding frequently. Customers will be confused by the inconsistency, which will also make long-term brand growth more challenging.

Starbucks is a good example of a brand.
Starbucks is the largest specialty coffee shop in the world, and its slogan has always promised to unite people.

The mission of Starbucks?

"To inspire and nurture the human spirit – one person, one cup, and one neighborhood at a time."

Because of this, every store offers free Wi-Fi, spacious tables, and calming music to make mingling with other customers simple. Your name is always written on your coffee as an added personal touch.

Despite removing the corporate name from the emblem in 2011, Starbucks' reputation as a strong brand has endured. What emotions do you have when you view that green mermaid logo? That must be something, I promise.

Be your company's strongest supporter and advice.
You (and your staff) are your brand's best promoters when you create a brand that works for your small business.
You are the expert on your brand, thus it is up to you to spread the word.

Be sure that the personnel you hire will fit into the purpose, vision, and values of your company.
Encourage staff members to create a personal brand that complements the process of establishing the brand of your business to expand reach.
Give your devoted clients a voice. Urge people to spread your material or provide reviews.

You are the expert on your brand, thus it is up to you to spread the word.

Now that you are aware of how to effectively create a brand, let's briefly review the elements required to properly lay the groundwork for a solid digital brand.

While developing brands for companies like yours, my brand firm focuses on these important aspects. Let's go over the methods for increasing brand recognition through advertising, social media, and community development.

User Experience on Websites
The most crucial marketing tool you have for expanding your company and creating a strong brand is your website.

Your customers will go here to find out more about your company and to take action when they're ready. To convert, not only must the user experience be top-notch, but your messaging also must convey the essence of your business.

When establishing your website for the first time, it's crucial to have everything in place, including the appropriate content management system, web hosting, and domain name registration.

Above all, your site must load quickly and be compatible with mobile devices (a responsive web design).
SEO and content are two of the most efficient long-term strategies for raising brand recognition for your website.
The bulk of your brand marketing initiatives will increase website visitors. In addition to a polished and gorgeously designed UI, your content must be interesting.

The next component of a strong digital brand strategy is SEO and content marketing, which leads us to our next point.

Content marketing and SEO
Search engine optimization (SEO) and the creation of relevant content are two of the most efficient long-term strategies to raise brand recognition and drive relevant organic traffic to your website.

It is possible to place yourself in search engine results in a variety of ways. Develop a thorough approach that takes into account the key elements of search engine positioning while also producing really valuable content that fulfills user intent.

The idea is that a clearly defined content marketing plan will enable you to engage with your target market and support them throughout their customer journey, so fostering brand loyalty that will ultimately lead to conversions.

Most significantly, your website's blog will always be the cornerstone of your SEO and content publication activities.
You should think about the following while creating a blog for your company:

Which material will be most appealing to your target market?
How can users find the information in organic search results?
When should publications be published with the best frequency and timing?
What strategy is being used to promote the content?

But, don't just stop at a blog! Infographics, videos, podcasts, case studies, whitepapers, lead magnets, and other forms of brand material are also possible.

Use of social media

Almost 74% of savvy customers utilize social networks to research brands before making a purchase!

How can your company use social media to better inform, connect, and interact with consumers and clients?

The following actions are examples of social media marketing best practices:

Curating pertinent content and putting out fresh material
Participation in community development
Paid promotion
A clear social media plan will make it easier to decide what has to be accomplished to strengthen ties with your community.

By providing pertinent, excellent content, any brand should be portrayed consistently across all social media platforms. Your goal with social media is to first earn the trust of your audience. then show loyalty. Then, promote the goods and services associated with your brand.

Emails sent to your list will have the greatest click-through rate. Never undervalue the effectiveness of list building in the beginning.

Email Promotion
Did you know that the emails you send to your list will have the greatest click-through rate? Don't undervalue the importance of list development while starting your brand-building campaign.

Consider your email marketing list to be your closest group of friends, and treat your subscribers accordingly.
On your website, you may use many opt-in forms to grow your subscriber base for your business, including:

Pop-Ups
Sidebars
Scroll Mats
Slide-ins
Lead magnet forms
Website Landing page

For your website to receive more traffic and for email conversions to rise, it is essential to deliver the appropriate material to the right person at the right time. Furthermore, because consumers are at various stages of the buying process, not every email should be sales-driven.

When focusing on particular audiences inside your marketing funnel, use the following email campaign kinds.

(Standard/Seasonal) promotions
Non-promotional (blog) (blog)
Newsletter
Greeting series
Drip campaign
Cart renunciation (ecommerce)
When statistics show that email marketing campaigns have an average ROI of $44 for every $1 spent, email is king!

Analytics reporting should always be in alignment with your company's strategic brand-building objectives and KPIs.

Paid Promotion
Creating a profitable paid advertising campaign for your brand has a special set of difficulties. Your pay-per-click (PPC) advertisements' total efficacy depends on a variety of factors.

A successful paid advertising campaign on websites like Facebook or Google Adwords significantly depends on:
intelligent advertising objectives
An established target market
Well-defined campaign structures
tracking performance with great care
captivating, original copy and design
Split-testing for improvement
Choosing appropriate keywords

Always keep in mind that paid advertising might completely deplete your budget.

Leads and sales might stop once the advertising does, too.
Paid advertising is alluring because it may produce immediate, short-term outcomes. Although it is unquestionably beneficial, for the best long-term return on investment, combine PPC with all of the aforementioned inbound marketing strategies.

Reports & Analytics
You should continue to keep track of important area development on a monthly and annual basis. With this information, you can adjust your brand-building and marketing efforts to best take

advantage of the strategies that provide the most potential.

Always support your company's strategic goals and KPIs in analytics reporting.
The fact that 75% of websites for small businesses don't employ analytics software to monitor performance always shocks me greatly.

Making sure Google Analytics is set up on your website should be your first step. You can get a ton of useful information on user habits with this free app. You may also create objectives to monitor conversions.

What is the goal of your brand? Create a concise statement that captures the core values of your business.

You now have a thorough understanding of the strategies used to increase brand recognition through marketing, engagement, and community development.
Each new or current firm may establish a strong brand in the digital era by combining all these elements with a plan and consistent execution.

In Conclusion: Building Your Company's Brand

One of the most important things you can do for your new or current business is branding.

A strong brand-building strategy may help your company go from a niche player to a formidable rival.

Customers will grow to trust your brand more deeply and be more inclined to buy what you have to offer, you'll find.

To support your objective, you must create a unified messaging and visual identity.
Include your brand in all facets of the consumer experience, including your retail, website, and interpersonal encounters.
Always begin by creating your brand strategy before anything else.

Bonus: Become your company's strongest supporter.
Remember that a brand is a story that is always being told.

Create a strong brand and share your story (Give me a review)

Chapter 6:

EXPANDING YOUR BUSINESS

It's difficult to grow your business. That requires a lot of work. It first entails donning several hats. Dealing with sales and marketing entails this. It entails being aware of business compliance and taxes. Daily consumer interaction is a requirement of the job. And a whole lot more. At the end of the day, you feel the effects of it.

There is hope for company owners who are having trouble expanding their enterprises. Indeed, it is difficult. What is the alternative, though? A 9-to-5 job that drains your life? For sure not. Alright, so perhaps you yearn for the stability of a steady wage. But at what psychological or emotional cost will that be paid?

The reality? You may easily find methods to expand your business and earn more money rapidly if you put in the effort, calm your mind, and just look at things from a different viewpoint. Although there are probably hundreds of business development techniques out there, the following will help your company grow rapidly and effectively.

There are several strategies to swiftly expand a firm. Some take a lot of time at first. That much is to be anticipated. Yet in the end, the advantages and earnings will make them more than worthwhile.

You must invest the time if you want to see results, just as with anything else in life or business. Don't concentrate on the immediate results of your job. Consider the long run. Provide genuine value and strive to assist your clients. care really. The first point needs to be that. Following that, scaling requires just that you take initiative and put in the necessary effort.

1. Create a sales funnel
Building a sales funnel is the first step in creating a firm that expands rapidly. You're doing yourself a grave disservice if your business doesn't have a sales funnel. Your business may be automated with the use of sales funnels. You can scale and develop rapidly and simply with its assistance. Yes, some front-end work is required. Obviously. But once those procedures are in place, everything goes well.

Before it is built, every sales funnel must be properly thought out. Focus first and primarily on the various funnels. For your business to scale and develop rapidly, whether it's a free-plus-shipping offer or a high-ticket coaching funnel, it's critical to establish your automated selling engine.

2. Make use of a client management program.
It's challenging to manually track transactions. Nobody wants to carry out it. When the firm expands, it becomes too onerous. Use a customer management system for easy scaling. There are several options available. Yet, a lot depends on the type of employment you do. Use what you find that works for you.

3. Examine the opposition.
You must study the competition before entering the market if you truly want to reach the broadest possible audience with your product. You get the opportunity to see through all of the ads, landing pages, and other funnel phases with x-ray vision.

You may discover any advertiser's online strategy with this. Pick the advertisements that have been running the longest and try to copy them. The easiest approach to scale any firm is in this manner. It's likely to work for you if it's tried-and-true and successful for your rivals.

4. Establish a patron loyalty program.

Loyalty programs are excellent tools for boosting sales. Gaining new consumers can be up to three times more expensive than selling to an established clientele. Some sources place this amount between four and ten times higher. Yet, getting new clients is pricey no matter how you look at it.

You can keep consumers by creating a customer loyalty program. It could also assist you in drawing in new customers. Long-term gains may be expected if there is a strong incentive for customers to spend more money with you. Create a compelling loyalty program, make it available to your current clientele, and watch your sales soar over time.

5. Discover fresh possibilities.
Assess new company chances by better comprehending your target market. Know everything, from your immediate competition to your distribution routes, and even how to analyze global markets and other possible sectors. With the right amount of research, you could probably explore hundreds of fresh options right away.

6. Create an email database.
Building an email list is one of the finest and most efficient methods to develop a business rapidly. It demonstrates categorically that you require a lead

magnet. Why else would anyone join your mailing list? A sales funnel is also required when using a lead magnet.

7. Create strategic alliances.

Strategic alliances with the appropriate businesses may change everything. It could let you immediately connect with a large number of customers. Finding those connections can be more difficult than it seems. Nonetheless, keep an eye out for businesses that match your own. Make contact with them and suggest joint venture ideas.

8. Use international platforms.

Selling things with an online store? Why not utilize Amazon FBA? a company that sells services? Why not employ Upwork? Are you engaged in the rental of holiday homes? Why not use worldwide networks like AirBnB, InvitedHome, HomeAway, etc.? Choose a platform that has achieved saturation to fast expand your business.

9. License agreements

Dealing with license agreements is a terrific method to expand your company without putting in a lot of extra work. A great strategy to expand rapidly is to have a product that you can license to others and participate in the profits. You may quickly reach market saturation by bringing a well-liked or profitable product to a large-scale business.

10. Consider a franchise model.

If your company is doing well and you want to expand it rapidly, think about franchising. Although switching to a franchise model is complicated and requires a lot of marketing expertise, it might make all the difference if you're searching for rapid development. Franchise fees are significant.

11. Expand the range of your offers.

Consider varying your offerings. What more goods, services, or data can you provide through your business? Consideration of growth is necessary if you want to advance. Find fresh chances within your specialized area. Find the trouble spots. What else might you offer your customers? Where else in the exchange can you provide value?

12. Create passive revenue sources.

A business must put up a lot of effort to grow. If your margins are tight, you might want to think about creating passive revenue sources. You won't have to worry as much, so to speak, about keeping the lights on this way. You will be able to make errors with passive income without having to lose everything. Offering you plenty of resources, will keep you in business and provide you with a foundation to expand, market, and scale swiftly.

13. Purchase additional companies.
Occasionally, purchasing other companies is a very rapid strategy to expand your own company. You may utilize them as platforms to grow quickly if you can locate rivals or companies in other sectors that would complement your own. Look both inside and outside of your sector for prospective business prospects.

14. Expansion internationally.
Can you reach a global audience? Can you grow up your current offers internationally? What would it take to conduct business in Europe, Canada, or Mexico? International expansion could be a rapid approach to growth if your offer converts. You'll pay some expenses. Sure. Yet there is a huge chance for financial gain.

15. Make a webinar
Webinars are a fantastic method to advertise any kind of good or service. Also, it might assist you in relatively quick business growth. With the help of webinars, you may immediately reach a large audience and promote practically any good or service. The webinar format is excellent for

capturing audiences and instantly closing transactions after sales.

UNDERSTANDING EXPANSION STRATEGIES

Stability strategies, expansion (growth), retrenchment, and combination strategies are frequently used to make judgments about the distribution of resources or follow an operational plan.
Each is discussed below.

A Stability Strategy is what?
A stable business strategy, as its name suggests, aims to sustain operations, market size, and position. This approach is typical of tiny, risk-averse businesses or businesses that are content with their existing position in a very unstable market.

These tactics may typically be divided into:

No Change Strategy - A company doesn't significantly alter its goals or operations. In its present operational and commercial context, the company analyzes the internal and external elements impacting it. The company decides consciously to keep its present strategic goals. This occurs most frequently when there is little competition, there have been no significant events that have shifted the market, and the firm's competitive position is solid. For instance, businesses that operate in niche markets frequently opt for a niche (cost or distinctiveness) strategy and stick with it until internal or external reasons make a change necessary.

Profit Strategies: A profit strategy is a set of guidelines that supports any actions required to uphold or increase profitability. Selling assets, boosting pricing, expanding output (sales), or making up losses with earnings from another company unit are a few examples of ways to reduce expenses (operational efficiency, outsourcing). This tactic is frequently used by profitable businesses that are now being threatened by short-term factors that might affect their profitability, such as competition, market conditions, recession, inflation, cost increases, etc. If these pressures persist, a profit strategy runs the risk of hurting the company by lowering competitiveness (particularly if the firm competes on cost or price). Before the business unit is dissolved or otherwise disposed of, the profit strategy may give short-term gains if a company's value offering or resources are becoming outdated. In any case, the tactic often does not entail the use of fresh resources. With the resources at their current levels or lower, profitability is maintained.

Cautionary Strategies: This approach calls for a company to wait and keep evaluating the market before implementing any specific tactics. Before making a strategic decision, it essentially serves as reconnaissance. While choosing a formal strategy to pursue, this is a temporary strategy that is used for a brief period. Until the company has a complete grasp of the market and the impact of previous strategies, it refrains from making any large resource investments and abandons any strategy formula it is pursuing. Manufacturing organizations frequently employ this tactic while assessing the introduction of new goods.

Expansion strategies: what are they?
A growth strategy is the same as an expansion plan. A company aims to develop more quickly, compete, make more money, build a stronger brand, take advantage of economies of scale, have a bigger effect, or take up more market share. This might mean expanding or enhancing present operations, entering new markets, focusing on new market segments, delivering new products or services, or

increasing market share through conventional competitive techniques.

The following are typical expansion techniques:

Growth by Concentration: This strategy includes concentrating operational effectiveness and resource allocation on one or a small number of key business units or functions. Concentration might involve generating a new value proposition to offer in the existing market, expanding an existing market by luring new consumers to an existing value proposition, or penetrating an existing market with an existing value proposition. One advantage of growth through concentration is that it enables the company to concentrate on markets where it already has operations and a certain degree of expertise. It is convenient to keep operations from changing significantly while utilizing current information. When it comes to putting too many eggs in one basket, this kind of technique might be problematic. The approach might fail due to modifications in the market (pricing changes, client mood, new value propositions, etc.).

Expansion through Diversification: This strategy entails expanding the company's value proposition through one of two channels: (1) Concentric

Diversification, which entails creating a new value proposition that is related to an existing value proposition, or (2) Conglomerate Diversification, which entails entering new markets (either with an existing value proposition or by combining with another industry competitor). This tactic often lowers certain industry risks, such as a downturn in the economy. During bad times, the earnings from one value offering may be able to make up for losses in another business unit.

Growth through Integration - To increase efficiency and provide economies of scale, integration entails the amalgamation of operational units anywhere along the value chain. It does not, however, call for altering current markets or focusing on new client demographics. The two main forms of integration are: (1) Vertical integration entails value chain consolidation at any point in the chain. Consolidating closer to the point where value is supplied to the consumer is known as forward vertical integration. Consolidating closer to the origin of value entails backward vertical integration (such as the point of manufacturing). Consolidating operations at the same point in the value chain is known as horizontal integration. This consolidation may take place between company units, through an acquisition of, or a merger with, a rival. For more information, see our separate discussion of horizontal and vertical integration.

Expansion through Collaboration: This tactic comprises closely collaborating with a rival (while potentially still competing against them in the market). Working together gives both firms a benefit that outweighs any benefit (or loss to the rival generated by not cooperating). Working together will often increase one or both rivals' operational efficiency or increase their market potential. Working together might take the shape of a joint venture, an affinity group or organization, a strategic alliance, or the consolidation of corporate divisions (mergers or acquisitions) (loose partnership-like alliance generally used to undertake a project or enter into foreign markets).

Internationalization-based expansion - entails finding new markets for a value proposition by going outside the immediate nation. In situations when there is minimal potential for domestic market development, this choice is often preferred. The aforementioned tactical methods can be used to internationalize:

(1) International strategy focuses on providing a value proposition in a foreign country without

changing its differentiation; (2) Multi-domestic strategy involves differentiating or modifying a product to appeal to or be suitable for foreign markets; (3) Global strategy concentrates on providing the standardized value proposition in nations with low delivery costs; and (4) Transnational Strategy uses both a global and a multi-domestic strategy.

What Do Retrenchment Strategies Entail?
Redeeming a business unit entails restructuring, selling, or some other kind of divestment. Costs are to be cut, processes are to be streamlined, or cash flow is to be stabilized. There are three main categories of retrenchment strategy:

Turnaround Strategy - This is a restructuring strategy. It demands realigning activities to be more lucrative or cost-effective. That frequently happens as a result of a bad strategy that hurts the business.
Reducing operations or fully divesting (getting rid of) a company entity are both parts of the divestment strategy. Often, the operational unit will be in the red or not align with the primary operational goals of the business. Negative cash flows, ongoing losses, inadequate company integration, better alternative uses of assets, the value offer becoming dated, rising expenses, or a

tiny (non-growing) market share are some of the factors driving this strategy. The company may now direct resources to a business segment that is more lucrative or strategically aligned. A divestiture typically occurs when a turnaround strategy has failed.

Liquidation Strategy - A liquidation strategy is similar to a divestment. It emphasizes the sale of certain assets or the closure of corporate divisions. In contrast to divestiture, which aims to focus resource allocation and streamline operations, liquidation considers a company unit to be a failure or a loss. Extensive losses, a lack of profitability, the failure of an existing strategy, outdated assets or technology, inadequate procedures, an outdated value proposition, bad management, or a lack of business unit integration are examples of scenarios that could lead to a liquidation strategy.

A Combination Strategy is what?
Any simultaneous combination of different master methods may be used in a combination strategy. It encompasses a company's adoption of many strategies in each of its business units, as well as the use of numerous strategies in a single business unit at one point or another. Large, complicated

organizations are where this is most prevalent (various industries and business units).

FRANCHISING AND OTHER EXPANSION MODELS

Entrepreneurs frequently find themselves at a crossroads over how to efficiently expand their business while limiting risk after years of successfully running a small firm. The next natural step is to increase your company's profile once your brand has demonstrated that its business strategy is sound and you have a following of devoted customers.

But, expanding your firm into new areas and moving it to the next level of success may be expensive. Owners must consider how much money is required to scale operations to satisfy the demands of the new markets they are trying to penetrate in addition to the cash required for company development.

Enter franchising: When faced with such a decision, franchising your company idea can be the best course of action for you. A crucial tactic for maximizing a company's market share is franchising. It's seen by many as a certain way for a flourishing company to expand without having to pay for it outright.

The potential to swiftly develop a business while avoiding risk and the need to acquire excessive cash or increasing expenses are two of franchising's most alluring features.

While franchising is a useful tool for organizations, it also presents both aspiring and seasoned entrepreneurs with a profitable business opportunity. By franchising, anyone may start their own business while receiving help and direction from a bigger organization that has a tested business strategy.

I'm here to walk you through the four main mechanics of franchising and how it may advance your company concept as the Chief Development Officer of a successful franchise brand with more than 365 sites across the United States.

1. Franchise may support localization and business diversification.
A business may remain local while still being scalable and consistent via franchising. As a business body, you can't easily accomplish this kind of development on your own.

The needs and feelings of the neighborhood are frequently well-known to new franchise owners who are planning to launch a facility there. The services of your business are made available to a larger audience through franchising expansion into new areas and regions, which diversifies and localizes your clientele.

2. There is not much risk involved in franchising.
It's not simple to launch a franchise or a stand-alone firm. Nonetheless, for both the franchisor and the franchisee, franchising an idea does significantly reduce the risk associated with starting or expanding a firm from scratch. Through franchising, the business owner may expand without compromising the caliber of their offerings, seeking outside funding, or raising overhead expenses.

Franchisees, on the other hand, profit from using a tried-and-true business strategy that has resources behind it. Naturally, starting a franchise is not something you can do quickly. Yet, franchising, as opposed to beginning a company from scratch, may provide business entrepreneurs with a launchpad and a support network to get going.

3. Strong franchisor-franchisee ties are essential.
Typically, franchisors give owners the training they need to run their businesses according to the franchise's business plan. Many do not need a degree or specialization to get started and also offer marketing guidance and mentoring. Franchises outperform start-up firms in terms of success rates.

85% of franchisees stay in business for five years or more, according to FranNet research. In contrast, just approximately 50% of businesses survive for five years or more. This information highlights the appeal of franchising for both business owners trying to grow and entrepreneurs searching for new opportunities.

4. Franchise offers chances to increase market share.
Franchising your idea may also assist your company's operations to run more smoothly and get a greater market share, enabling it to serve a wider range of clientele. For instance, BrightStar Care provides personal, skilled, and companion care as well as medical staffing for institutions and National Accounts, which are joint ventures between insurance companies and other healthcare providers that depend on our agencies for care services.

While home care and medical staffing have been a component of our business strategy since the beginning, franchising our idea in 2005 allowed us to expand our reach and, as a result, broaden the range of services we offer. Franchises provide businesses the chance to diversify their revenue streams and perhaps increase their earnings to an unlimited level.

Are franchises the best choice for you?

Franchising is a fantastic option that can help propel your brand into its next development phase if your local firm is financed for expansion and you have mechanisms in place that can be replicated at scale. Make no mistake: franchising is not a shortcut to development; expansion is a drawn-out and complicated process. Expanding on your present presence, increasing your market share, and reaching new consumers is an effective technique.

Chapter 7:

MANAGING YOUR WEALTH

The success of every investor depends on having a well-diversified portfolio. As an individual investor, you must understand how to choose an asset mix that best fits your unique investment objectives and risk tolerance. In other words, your portfolio should provide you with peace of mind while meeting your future cash needs. By using a systematic process, investors may build portfolios that are in line with their investing plans. Here are a few crucial actions for using such a strategy.

In general, your best chance for the continuous long-term growth of your assets is a well-diversified portfolio.

Choose the optimal asset mix for your investment objectives and risk tolerance first.

Choose the specific assets for your portfolio in the second step.

Finally, keep an eye on the portfolio's diversity and check to see whether weightings have altered.

Adjust as needed, choosing which underweighted securities to purchase using the money received from the sale of the overweighted assets.

Step 1: Determining Your Appropriate Asset Allocation

The first step in building a portfolio is to determine your unique financial condition and aspirations. Age, the amount of time you have to build your assets, the number of funds to invest, and future income requirements are crucial factors to take into account. A 55-year-old married individual intending to help pay for a child's college education and retire in the following ten years requires a different investing approach than an unmarried 22-year-old college graduate just starting their career.

Your personality and risk tolerance are further elements to take into account. Are you prepared to take a chance on maybe losing some money in exchange for a chance at bigger rewards? Everyone wants to earn big returns every year, but if you find it difficult to fall asleep when your investments experience a temporary decline, likely, the high returns from those sorts of assets are not worth the worry.

How your assets should be distributed among various asset classes will be determined by your current status, your future demands for cash, and your risk tolerance. The risk/return tradeoff concept states that the potential for higher rewards comes at the cost of a higher risk of losses. Instead of minimizing risk, you should seek to maximize it for your unique position and way of life. For instance, a young individual who won't need to rely on assets for income may afford to take bigger risks in the pursuit of high returns. The individual who is approaching retirement, on the other hand, has to concentrate on safeguarding their assets and obtaining income from these assets in a tax-efficient manner.

Aggressive vs. Conservative Investors
Your portfolio will typically be more aggressive and allocate a higher part to stocks and less to bonds and other fixed-income assets the more risk you are willing to take on. On the other hand, your portfolio will be more cautious with the less risk you can take.

A conservative portfolio's primary objective is to preserve value. The proposed allocation would produce current income from the bonds and also offer some opportunity for long-term capital gain from the investment in high-quality stocks.

Step 2: Develop the Portfolio

You must allocate your capital among the relevant asset classes once you have chosen the ideal asset mix. This is not complicated at all; stocks are stocks and bonds are bonds.

But, you may further divide the various asset classes into subclasses, each of which has a unique set of risks and possible rewards. An investor may, for instance, distribute the equity element of the portfolio across firms with various market capitalizations, different industrial sectors, and both local and international equities. The bond component may be divided between short-term and long-term bonds, government debt and business debt, and so on.

You may implement your asset allocation plan in several ways (be sure to consider the quality and potential of each asset you invest in), including:

Stock selection - Choose equities for the equity element of your portfolio that meet the degree of risk you wish to handle; take into account the sector, market cap, and stock type. Use stock screeners to analyze the firms to narrow down probable purchases, and then perform more thorough research on each potential buyer to identify its prospects and hazards moving ahead.

This method of adding stocks to your portfolio needs the greatest work since it calls for you to continuously monitor price fluctuations in your assets and keep up with business and industry news.

Bond selection - There are several things to take into account when selecting bonds, including the coupon, maturity, bond type, credit rating, and the overall interest-rate environment.

Mutual Funds - You can own stocks and bonds that have been carefully chosen and researched by fund managers by investing in mutual funds, which are available for a variety of asset classes. Of course, the fees that fund managers charge for their services will reduce your returns. Another option is index funds, which are passively managed and typically have lower costs since they replicate an established index.

Exchange-Traded Funds (ETFs) - If you'd rather not use mutual funds for your investments, ETFs can be a good substitute. To put it simply, ETFs are mutual funds that trade like stocks. They are comparable to mutual funds in that they own a broad assortment of stocks that are often categorized by sector, capitalization, nation, and other factors. Yet, they are different in that they follow a selected index or another collection of equities rather than being actively managed. ETFs provide diversity while being less expensive than mutual funds since they are passively managed. ETFs are a great way to diversify your portfolio since they offer exposure to a wide range of asset types.

Step 3: Reevaluating Portfolio Weightings

After your portfolio is in place, you should frequently review it and rebalance it since changes in price movements may cause your original weightings to shift. Calculate the investments' relative values to the total and objectively classify them to get your portfolio's real asset allocation.

Your present financial condition, future demands, and risk tolerance are other considerations that might change over time. You might need to modify your portfolio if these factors alter. You might need to own fewer stocks if your risk tolerance has decreased. Or maybe your asset allocation dictates that a modest part of your assets be invested in riskier small-cap companies since you're now ready to take on additional risk.

Find out which of your positions are overweighted and underweighted to rebalance. Say, for instance, that your asset allocation indicates that you should only have 15% of your assets in small-cap shares, but you already have 30% of such securities. Choosing how much of this position to diminish and distribute to other classes is part of the rebalancing process.

Step 4: Strategic Rebalancing

Choose which underweighted securities you will purchase with the money from selling the overweighted securities after determining which securities you need to decrease and by how much. Use the methods covered in Step 2 to select your securities.

Think about the tax ramifications of selling assets at this specific time while rebalancing and altering your portfolio.

If you were to sell all of your equity investments to rebalance your portfolio, even if your growth stock investment may have increased significantly over the last year, you may be subject to hefty capital gains taxes. In this situation, it could be more advantageous to simply stop making future contributions to that asset class while carrying on with contributions to other asset classes. This will gradually decrease the percentage of growth stocks in your portfolio without triggering capital gains taxes.

Always keep in mind your securities' view at the same time. Notwithstanding the tax repercussions, you might wish to sell those same overweighted growth companies if you believe they are ominously about to collapse. Research papers and analyst forecasts may be helpful tools for assessing the prospects for your assets. Also, you might use the tax-loss selling approach to lessen the tax impact.

conclusion

You must prioritize keeping your diversification throughout the whole process of building your portfolio. You must diversify within each asset class in addition to merely owning assets from each one. Make sure your investments in a particular asset class are dispersed throughout a variety of subclasses and industrial sectors.

As we previously discussed, using mutual funds and ETFs allows investors to attain good diversification. With the help of these investment vehicles, small-dollar individual investors can benefit from the same economies of scale as institutional investors and huge fund managers.

TAX PLANNING STRATEGIES

Your financial circumstances, including how much money you make, how you make it, and how your spending is organized, will determine how much tax you owe. Your tax bill will change if you alter any of those factors. Look at which of those facts you can and are prepared to modify in a way that will decrease your bill if you want to cut your taxes.

These factual modifications are effective tax planning techniques. These entail looking at your existing financial status to find chances to increase your tax efficiency. Create a system that lets you keep more of your money so you can accumulate wealth quicker by developing a tax plan. Your wealth strategy and your tax plan should be coordinated.

The present is the ideal opportunity to alter your facts. Regardless of when you read this, you still have time to make changes that might reduce your taxes for the current fiscal year.

For those wishing to alter their taxes by manipulating the facts, the following tax planning options are provided:

1. USE YOUR INCOME SMARTLY.

The amount of tax you pay is significantly influenced by how you generate your income. Governments in the majority of nations encourage company ownership, real estate investment, and the production of commodities like food and energy. Legislators designed tax regulations so that these producer activities are taxed at significantly lower rates than the typical incomes of the majority of consumers since these activities encourage economic growth.

Analyzing how you make money should be a key component of your tax preparation approach. Find possibilities that appeal to you so you may transition from being a consumer to a producer. You'll be able to keep more of the money you make and hasten the process of becoming wealthy.

You will have more control over when you recognize your income from a tax year perspective as you have greater control over how much money you make. It's a prevalent misconception that deferring revenue to a later year to lower your taxable income for the current tax year is always preferable. Accelerating your revenue might occasionally be a better strategic choice. If you are a company owner, maintain your revenue and distributions on track throughout the year to support your tax planning approach.

Review your situation with your tax advisor. They will discuss a few things with you, such as if cutting your income now results in you losing any of your allowable deductions and whether you expect tax rates to rise in the upcoming year.

2. EVALUATE YOUR ENTITIES.

Establishing an entity for your company is one of the finest strategies for cutting taxes since it is what we refer to as an organization created to do business. Choosing the correct asset to add to your portfolio at the right time can result in annual tax savings of up to $10,000 or more.

Residents in states with high taxes, such as New York, California, New Jersey, Illinois, Wisconsin, and Connecticut, place a greater emphasis on certain entities. You could find it more advantageous in some circumstances to pay more tax as a business than as a person.

The tough thing is that all entity forms are taxed differently, so it is crucial to pick carefully and make a strategy. Your tax expert can assist you in deciding if your organization should be taxed as a partnership, S Corp, C Corp, or self-employed.

Entrepreneurs frequently start a business as one kind of entity intending to switch to another type when the company has made a particular amount of money. But, in the rush of running a growing business, it's simple to forget to make the changeover. One error might cost you money.

Reviewing your entities annually should be a component of your tax planning approach. Your taxes and the process of preparing your tax return can be considerably impacted by the addition or removal of an organization, a change in status or ownership, or any of these events.

3. EVALUATE YOUR ACCOUNTING PROCESS.
The accrual technique or the cash method can be used for accounting by business owners whose annual gross revenue is less than $25 million. Cash accounting requires you to record money as soon as it is received and costs as soon as they are paid. While using accrual accounting, revenue is recognized as earned and costs as incurred.

The cash approach often provides the firm with additional tax advantages, however, this isn't always the case, so consult your tax professional. If you're switching, be aware that there are elections and forms to complete.

4. USE GOOD BOOKKEEPING PRACTICES.

Bookkeeping has a poor reputation. High achievers frequently view bookkeeping as tiresome, monotonous labor; even those who understand its significance rarely think about it first. However one of the finest techniques for lowering taxes is precise and timely bookkeeping.

Make sure your bookkeeping procedure is up to standard as part of your tax preparation approach. This comprises:

reconciling the accounts on your balance sheet
checking for mistakes in your profit and loss statement and balance sheet
If you keep up with this, you'll probably find new tax deductions you may claim, and you'll also be prepared for a simpler tax filing procedure.

5. MAINTAIN CURRENT DOCUMENTATION.

Make careful to extend appropriate documentation to other areas of your organization while you work on your bookkeeping. The most effective technique to back up your assertions and provide your tax adviser additional ammunition to aid you with your tax planning plans is with proper documentation. Also, proper documentation gives you the backing you'll need in the event of an audit.

Documentation could consist of:

Receipts
meeting records for your organizations
loan agreements between you and your firms or enterprises
Agreements that you have with your companies or other entities
Distance logs
Activity logs (especially for individuals who identify as "real estate professionals" in the U.S.

6. ANALYZE PERSONAL LOANS AND BUSINESS-RELATED EXPENSES.

Many individuals are unaware that taking money out of a company or piece of real estate in the guise of a legitimate loan is one technique to lawfully avoid paying taxes. The loan money obtained in this manner is not taxed. Make sure the loan is properly documented and that you pay the principal and interest as specified in the loan by working with your adviser to ensure that these things happen.

Moreover, make sure you properly report any business costs for reimbursement if you paid them out of pocket (regardless of whether you own the firm. Make sure you are paid back if you don't own the company. However, if you own the company, you could be missing out on a tax break. Check with your tax adviser about any unreimbursed expenditures you may have to determine if there are any options for you to claim them as a personal deduction.

7. REMEMBER TO TAKE DEDUCTIONS.
Since they don't take full use of their available deductions, many people pay more tax each year than they are required to.

Some people just don't seize the chance. If that is you, the tips for enhancing your paperwork to include all of your possible deductions are in #2 above.

Nonetheless, a startlingly high percentage of people intentionally forgo part or all of their allowable deductions out of fear. What causes their phobias? a tax audit. They have voluntarily given up deductions because they were informed that certain of them trigger IRS suspicions.

Your financial situation quickly improves when you take the proper tax deductions and support yourself with the necessary paperwork.

Among the most frequently overlooked deductions are:

office at home. It's not a good idea for everyone to claim a home office deduction. But, there are also situations when the deduction is what takes you beyond the standard deduction limit. Also, working from home gives you additional possibilities to write off your vehicle expenditures. Plan your best course of action with the help of your tax counselor. the pass-through deduction of 20%. This deduction, which was added to the tax code in 2017, can help small businesses save a lot of money.
Bonus depreciation for syndicators and real estate investors. Since 2018, investors have had the option to either stretch out or take bonus depreciation in one big amount. You should carefully examine this deduction as part of your tax planning strategy to identify the best course of action. In some circumstances, the majority of a property may be depreciated in the year of purchase.

8. EVALUATE YOUR GIVING.

Gaining more financial freedom so they may donate more to causes they care about is a big element of the appeal of wealth accumulation for many people. If you manage the gifts following the tax code, charitable donations can also be a way to lower your taxes.

Be sure the organizations you choose to accept donations from are recognized as nonprofit 501(c)(3) organizations when you plan and evaluate your giving as part of your tax planning approach (3). If so, consult your tax expert to determine if the organization is still eligible for tax deductions in some other method, such as by gifts to certain trusts and churches. Make sure your counsel considers both because many states also provide tax incentives for charitable donations.

You can claim a charitable deduction even if you don't provide money. You can contribute cash, in-kind services, or other tangible items. For instance, based on their fair-market value, company owners can deduct contributions of desks, computers, or other equipment. A formal appraisal is required for donations of property valued at $5,000 or more, which frequently involves jewels, collectibles, and real estate. Discuss the appropriate manner to record these sorts of donations with your tax counselor. If you want to donate shares instead of cash, your adviser can also offer advice.

Lastly, a lot of business owners want to instill a philanthropic mindset as one of their core beliefs. Giving employees paid time off to participate in the community or organizing a day of company-wide service are two examples of this kind of project. Business owners in these situations can work with their tax experts to document these occurrences and deduct the compensation, perks, and other costs related to that period.

9. COMPREHEND HOW SALES AND PURCHASES OF PROPERTY AFFECT YOUR TAXES.

Your taxes may be impacted by investments in equipment, cars used for business, and rental property. You can generate significant savings potential by incorporating a discussion of these matters in your tax planning approach with your tax professional.

You can legitimately avoid paying taxes, for instance, by engaging in a like-kind exchange with your real estate acquisitions. This method is selling a piece of property and then using the money to acquire another one to avoid paying taxes on the property you just sold.

Although not every transaction results in a deduction, almost every transaction has the possibility of one. You may generate significant savings throughout your life by viewing your transactions through the lens of your tax planning approach.

10. THINK ABOUT HIRING YOUR YOUNGER KIDS.
The benefits of working with your children are numerous. First, the business can deduct their compensation from taxes. The tax code rewards you for creating a job with a deduction.

Secondly, they'll probably pay less tax on their income than you do. In the US, children have a tax bracket of 10 to 12 percent, which is far lower than that of their income-earning parents, and a standard deduction of $12,000. The first $12,000 may be tax-free, and any additional income may be taxed at this reduced rate if you run a business and can lawfully employ them and pay them a wage. By investing a portion of their income in a 529 college savings plan, your kid can minimize their tax liability if they do end up having to pay taxes.

This is a smart way for some families to teach kids the importance of working in the family company while also helping them save money for the future.

There are several factors to consider when developing a tax planning strategy. With the help of your adviser, carefully examining your present tax information is a terrific method to find a way to consistently save a lot of money.

ASSET PROTECTION STRATEGIES

Recognize that asset assurance has nothing to do with deceiving your lenders to avoid paying your obligations. Instead, it has to do with defending your well-earned or acquired riches from financial vultures and insignificant claims.

The following list of 10 asset protection techniques should help you protect your wealth.

1. Use corporate entities
If you are a business visionary, you should separate your assets from your company's assets. A business problem might cause you to lose everything if you don't figure out how to create distinct business

components, such as limited liability firms, organizations, or limited associations.

Among the business factors to take into account are:

single-person business
restrictive partnership
common partnership
Limited-risk enterprise
Corporation

2. Raise Your Liability Insurance Level

Your first line of defense against any foreseeable prosecution should be obligation protection. Risk management safeguards you from unfounded claims filed against your company or alleged injuries that occurred at work.

These wounds include actual physical ones that resulted from tripping and falling, defamation, or employees making untrue claims. Increase your obligation limit if you recently received a settlement or legacy.

It seems sensible to get an individual umbrella liability insurance policy that covers you for as much as or more than your new total assets.

Before receiving the settlement or legacy, be sure you have it.

3. Employ retirement accounts.
In the event of bankruptcy, government legislation provides unlimited asset insurance to Registered Retirement Savings Plans. The amount of assets that are guaranteed, however, differs between regions, with some providing greater certainty than others.

To determine how much certainty you may obtain from using retirement funds, look into the legislation in your area.

4. Establish A irrevocable Trust
By using trusts, you may also protect yourself from loan managers. The ideal kind of trust is an irreversible one, which denotes that the terms cannot be changed once the trust has been established.

Also, if you transfer assets to this trust, they will no longer be regarded as your property and instead become the property of the trust. This prevents creditors from pursuing these assets.

5. Exemptions for Property

Several areas guarantee the value of homes. This suggests that if you choose not to pay, the law will prevent the court from awarding your lenders the value of your house. Nonetheless, the assessment of house worth made sure that there were changes in territory.

Some provide almost no insurance in the event of bankruptcy, while others provide an unlimited amount. If you want to be certain about this, look into the legislation in your region.

6. Place certain assets in the name of your spouse
If one spouse works in a dangerous field or leads a dangerous lifestyle, it makes sense to put some of their assets in the other spouse's name. The lenders of one partner are frequently prohibited from pursuing the other partner's other properties.

In this way, marriage may be used as a method of asset insurance, allowing significant assets to be retained as the sole property of the couple with little exposure to risk. Prenuptial or postnuptial property arrangements are useful in certain circumstances.

It is indicated that you should use caution while putting this strategy into practice. Although it is a practical way to protect your property from loan officers, it will affect how your assets are divided if you were to somehow end up separating.

7. Life insurance and annuities
A lot of assurance is provided in some areas for annuity adjustments and assets in real money value life insurance. Again, every region has its unique rules in this regard.

8. Think about Tenancy By The Entirety
In a few places, you might refer to your living situation as tenancy by the whole. The implication is that the property cannot be added to or separated by the claim if one life partner is sued.

Using this method has further advantages in that it is founded on legal principles. This means that you won't need to spend a lot of money to complete and maintain the task.

9. Don't Show Off Your Wealth
There is a reason why a considerable portion of the allegations is made against those who have substantial financial resources. Glimmering your money invites financial vultures to file a lawsuit against you.

Remember that extravagant displays of riches tend to inspire more yearning than deep reverence. Being wealthy is wiser than appearing wealthy.

10. Aim to protect yourself right away.
When a claim is inevitable, the aforementioned processes cannot be started. The courts will view this as suspicious behavior, and they can forbid you from transferring your assets to classes that are guaranteed, leaving your assets exposed.

Start carrying out these actions in this manner as soon as you can.

Conclusion
The information provided here is by no means an exhaustive guide to protecting your possessions. This theme has a wide range of complex variables because each scenario is unique. The most important thing is to move as soon as your money is threatened.

Unfortunately, there is a stigma associated with offshore asset protection that suggests illegal or evasive financial management. When carried out properly, asset protection is undoubtedly legal, thus we strongly advise completing your study and seeing a counselor as needed.

One platform, Business Setup Worldwide, has the answers to all of your queries. Call us right away with any questions. We would be delighted to assist.

APPRECIATION

"Dear Reader,

Thank you for choosing to read 'Building Your own Wealth: The Ultimate Guide to Achieving Personal Finance'. I wrote this book with the hope of sharing valuable insights and strategies that can help you achieve financial freedom.

I would like to take a moment to express my gratitude for your interest and investment in this book. I believe that you will find the content of this book to be both informative and practical.

If you have found this book helpful, I would be grateful if you could take a few moments to leave an honest review on my Amazon page.
Your feedback would not only help me understand what worked for you, but also help other readers who are looking for a similar book. I am confident that your review will be a valuable asset to anyone considering purchasing the book.

Thank you for considering my request. I hope you find this book to be a valuable resource for years to come.

www.ingramcontent.com/pod-product-compliance
Lightning Source LLC
Chambersburg PA
CBHW071133220526

45467CB00015B/923